REBUILDING
THE
RUINS
OF
REGRET

Why the Rubble of Your Worst Decisions
of the Past Can Become the
Foundation of Your Greatest Future

REBUILDING THE RUINS OF REGRET

P. G. FINLEY

ARROWS & STONES

Copyright © 2024 by P.G. Finley

Published by Arrows and Stones

All rights reserved. No portion of this book may be reproduced, stored in a retrieval system, or transmitted in any form or by any means—electronic, mechanical, photocopy, recording, scanning, or other—except for brief quotations in critical reviews or articles, without prior written permission of the author.

Unless otherwise noted, all Scripture is taken from the Holy Bible, New International Version®, NIV®. Copyright © 1973, 1978, 1984, 2011 by Biblica, Inc.™ Used by permission of Zondervan. All rights reserved worldwide. www.zondervan.com. The "NIV" and "New International Version" are trademarks registered in the United States Patent and Trademark Office by Biblica, Inc.™ | Scripture quotations marked AMP are taken from the Amplified® Bible (AMP), Copyright © 2015 by The Lockman Foundation. Used by permission. www.lockman.org | Scripture quotations marked ESV are from The ESV® Bible (The Holy Bible, English Standard Version®), copyright © 2001 by Crossway, a publishing ministry of Good News Publishers. Used by permission. All rights reserved. | Scripture quotations marked NLV are from The New Life Version® Bible, Copyright © 1969, 2003 by Barbour Publishing, Inc.

For foreign and subsidiary rights, contact the author.

Cover design by: Sara Young
Cover photo by: Andrew van Tilborgh

ISBN: 978-1-962401-29-6   1 2 3 4 5 6 7 8 9 10

Printed in the United States of America

*To those who forced me to take a hard
look in the mirror thus allowing me to
see who God created me to be.*

CONTENTS

Foreword ix

Acknowledgments xi

Introduction 13

HARD TRUTH #1 **It Will Not and Cannot Work.** 31

HARD TRUTH #2 **Retain Your Honor and Good Name at All Costs.**

It May Be All You Have. 43

HARD TRUTH #3 **Guilt Can Make You Do Bad Things.** 57

HARD TRUTH #4 **Holidays Suck.** 71

HARD TRUTH #5 **A Beautiful Woman Can Pull Your Puppet Strings.** ... 85

HARD TRUTH #6 **You Will Never Keep Up with the Jones's.**

They Can't Even Keep Up with Themselves. 105

HARD TRUTH #7 **Rip Off the Band-Aid.** *You Can't Escape Your Reality.* . . 119

HARD TRUTH #8 **Learn Your Purpose and True Nature.**

And Resist the Voices of Outside Influences. 133

HARD TRUTH #9 **Reject the Labels and Dare to Speak Your Truth.** 149

HARD TRUTH #10 **People <u>WILL ALWAYS</u> Watch You.** 163

Afterword 175

FOREWORD

I have had the privilege of walking with P.G. Finley for over twelve years as he has fought through many battles. The pain of each battle would have taken most men down, but he was not going to give in and be taken down. He has been persistent in pressing into a relationship with God and discovering the purpose for each battle, gaining wisdom from his mistakes and failures. From the beginning, God showed me who he was. As he embraced who God created him to be, he gained more strength and wisdom that he shares in this book. How we view life depends on our relationship with God. As he began to seek more understanding of how he got where he was and the consequences of his bad decisions, God allowed him to view his life through the Scripture: *"All things work together for good for those who love God and are called according to His purpose"* (Romans 8:28, paraphrase).

P.G. Finley discovered that you have to fight for something greater than yourself to achieve victory over your problems. The purpose you were born for is worth fighting for. God has called him to help men face the truth behind their pain and struggles and seek God to find the greater purpose. Pain is a part of life. Many people medicate their pain while others run from pain only to look behind and see it's a repeated pattern following close behind them. He discovered that freedom comes as you face the deep-rooted pain behind your struggles. He will inspire you to stop running and face the ten "Hard Truths" spelled out clearly in this book. His pursuit of purpose is impressive and inspiring, and he will challenge you to face these truths and seek God for the greater purpose you were born for so that you too can impact the world around you.

—Pastor Denise Boggs
Living Waters Ministry

ACKNOWLEDGMENTS

With all things in this world, nobody can achieve greatness alone. First, I would like to thank my children. All three of you witnessed firsthand the difficulties I faced and the emotions that ensued with each stone removed from a broken heart. I pray that you find even in the darkest places, a glimmer of hope that you can transform your life into one of fulfillment, success, and peace.

Next, I would like to thank my parents and siblings. You listened to me and gave insight that was valuable in helping me believe that I was not the circumstances surrounding me.

To Living Waters Ministry—the relationships, counseling, and guidance I received gave me the fuel and desire to write for something bigger than I even imagined on my healing journey and the creation of this book.

To Pastor Denise and Pastor Paul—you had the insight to speak it plain and harsh at times to get through my thick skull by speaking the truth even when I did not want hear it.

To my velociraptor—you were no help in actually writing this book but by sitting next to me for countless hours, it forced me to concentrate so that I would not disturb you, which would ensure nothing got done.

To my God—You are my creator. It is my hope that this story will help countless other "prodigal sons" find their way back to the purpose You put in the hearts.

INTRODUCTION

Hello, manipulators and self-serving individuals...
Habakkuk 2:2: "*Write down the revelation and make it plain on tablets so that a herald may run with it.*"

"If you do not change your life, you will be alone, broke, and living under a bridge." This simple sentence has stuck with me for years. Even at the height of my pride, this nugget of truth has resonated inside of me like a song that you cannot get out of your head, a song that can irritate you but is catchy at the same time. You find yourself singing to it but can never allow anyone to hear you. A song that if anyone knew you could recite each lyric like breathing, you could reveal something about yourself that you do not want anyone knowing. Something that, if known, could destroy the outward appearance of the person you have painted to the world. I am writing this book to tell you, it's time to tear down the veil of your false life and enter into the life God created you for. Otherwise, if you continue on your current path, you will have to decide:: do you like your master bedroom with or without a water view? Based upon today's home prices and interest rates, your bridge most likely will be under an interstate overpass with a beautiful waterfall of oil and grime dripping into your cardboard box.

This book is a look into a realm that other books have touched upon but have never given life to. The ugly side of your decisions. The things of what are to become or have already become. Like the ghosts in Charles Dickens' classic, *A Christmas Carol*, you will be visited by three of them.[1] We will discuss in detail the past, present, and future. The past is what led you to where you are. It is no accident that this book is in your hands. The script of your life has been written without you knowing it. However, the time for ownership of your life will need to be accepted and placed in your hands. Let's start simple but matter of fact: you are where you are based on your decisions and yours alone. You cannot blame anyone for where you currently are. The present is how your decisions are affecting your current life—the struggles you face, the lack of peace, or the uselessness you feel. Likewise, the future is what is yet to be written, including the person you want to become but perhaps are not sure how to get there in the current mess you are in. The stories that will be presented, using real examples, will highlight and bring to light the predictability of some decisions you may encounter. By opening the door to my mistakes, I hope to help you live the life God has always desired for you to live.

Cooking is easy. You read a recipe and scavenge the pantry to see if you have the ingredients. If you do, you measure and cook according to the instructions given to you. If not, you go to the store, buy the ingredients, and then cook according to the instructions given to you. So simple, right? When everything is written out for you, the simplicity of following directions should be apparent. Nevertheless, why do people fail at following

---

[1] Charles Dickens, A Christmas Carol (Strand, London: Chapman & Hall, 1843).

instructions? Why do recipes with five-star reviews taste so bad? Perhaps we measured wrong, or the food was not fresh. How about when we forgot something was in the oven and burned the top of the cheese? Even when something is precise and leaves no room for mistakes, mistakes find their way to spoiling our best intentions and destroying something that was meant to be pleasurable. Using this logic, let us apply this to life.

A baby is not born with an instruction manual on how to assemble into adulthood. No Pinterest recipe tells us that if we add two tablespoons of love, one cup of praise, a pinch of success, and bake it for twenty years, the perfect person will arise. The thought of this is comical but most people believe this is how you should live life. If a person messes up, no recipe states: Step 1: Pray. Step 2: Apologize. Step 3: Repair and all things will be perfect. Although each of these steps has a place in living your best life, this cookbook approach will keep you locked in your current state and unable to ascend to an individual of character and virtue. News flash, life is not an Ikea product. There is no single hexagon wrench that can fix or put back together our lives after a mistake. Likewise, a single apology or following a self-help book does not always heal our marriages, make us amazing parents, or prevent us from ever going astray from God's perfect plan again.

Writing was never something I enjoyed growing up. My favorite subjects were math, history, and science. Like most boys, English/literature was more feminine and to say you enjoyed reading somehow made you less of a man, or so we thought. When we wanted to learn (and that was not often), I can assure you, we wanted to know how we could blow something up in chemistry class, not whether this poem was an iambic pentameter. Honestly, who really cared how some dead guy wrote something that was irrelevant to my life. Many years go by and a ridiculous amount of schooling forces me to read and write more and more frequently. The idea of blowing something up begins to fade and I begin to realize that reading speaks to something deeper inside. I begin to slowly understand that reading releases my mind from physical constraints. It forces me out of the grind of everyday life and takes me to a place that no movie, podcast, or TikTok video can replace. I began to understand that reading challenges me to evaluate my inner thoughts and dusts the cobwebs out of my mind, thus allowing clarity. In addition, it helps me focus on things that remain elusive. By doing this, it makes my mind stronger so I can peel back the layers of crap that have formed, clouding my ability to be the man God called me to be.

Quite honestly, writing this book is nothing short of a miracle. Maybe it's not quite bringing the dead back to life, but perhaps it is turning water into wine. When I was told I would write this seven years ago, I had the typical response that most of you would have, "There is no way in hell. You realize I am the least qualified for this." I have zero formal training in writing. I am not a pastor, preacher, professor, journalist, sportswriter, or poet. I was divorced. I was a selfish womanizer who only cared about advancing his career so that I could impress people. Likewise, I was in debt, despite making a very good paycheck. If I am going to write a book on how not to live, then I am your man. So, one day at a time, I began to put to words what I was thinking. Like an ancient poet, I began to write my tragedies and gave form to my mishaps. The end product is what you are about to read, and hopefully, with an open mind. So let me start by explaining the what, the why, the who, and the how of this book.

WHAT MAKES THIS BOOK UNIQUE, NOT ORIGINAL?

I learned a long time ago that you cannot encourage everyone. Regardless of what you do, someone is not going to like your actions, and that is okay. Regardless of what you say, someone is not going to receive from you, and that is okay. Regardless of your intentions, someone is not going to believe you have their best interest at heart, and that is okay. As Steve Jobs once said, "If you want to make everyone happy, don't be a leader—sell ice cream."[2] With that in mind, I realize this book will not be for everyone. First, it will contain real stories and consequences of my actions in the rawest form. In doing this, I hope to make you feel uncomfortable and find yourself saying, "How did you not see that coming?" Likewise, it will force you to examine your own life and actions through a lens that takes you out of your current situation. It will give you the opportunity to examine the pattern of your choices and link them to a very real aftermath that may follow.

Second, it will be written in a non-traditional form from what you are used to. I will not be quoting scripture on every page because frankly, I do not know them. I spent years running from the truth and it is through His grace that I survived and thrived. He has spoken to me through His word but for me to quote His word and know the address of where to find it, and that is a stretch. Many of us are like this, and guess what? It is okay. God

---

[2] Steve Jobs, "Steve Jobs once said, 'If you want to make everyone happy, don't be a leader, sell ice cream,'" LinkedIn, 7 April, 2021, https://www.linkedin.com/pulse/steve-jobs-once-said-you-want-make-everyone-happy-dont-ali-abdellah.

wants your heart for Him, and your ability to quote scripture for the world to see is irrelevant. As I stated earlier, I am not a pastor or theologian. I never went to seminary and the thought of a book like that would not appeal to the intended audience, as you have probably strayed so far that constant scripture quoting might cause you to lose interest. The goal is for you to follow the journey, good and bad, through my own story that you will be able to relate to regardless of where you are in your life.

> HOW FAR YOU ARE YOU WILLING TO WALK OUT OF YOUR COMFORT ZONE AND REALLY CHALLENGE ALL THAT SEEMS NATURAL TO YOU WILL CREATE SMALL VICTORIES AND THEN BIGGER ONES.

Third, this book will be bold and tough. It will challenge you to examine the deepest parts of your soul to find your strength and unlock your true self. You will realize that this is a fight. A fight for your family, friends, and self. A fight that if you declare you will succeed, anything is possible. However, success will be determined by how deep you are willing to go. How far you are willing to walk out of your comfort zone and really challenge all that seems natural to you will create small victories and then bigger ones. It will highlight how certain battles are irrelevant and just drain your energy to fight the true battles that will turn the war in your favor.

Through writing this book, I was constantly reminded of a spider web. A spider web is a very intricate array of silk that is arranged in a pattern and used to trap its prey. Every night a spider goes out and spends time weaving this web to catch food. It waits patiently for an unsuspecting bug to fly right into what it cannot see. Once there, the web holds the insect until the spider is ready to eat. Likewise, our strongholds and enemies do the same to us. We get so caught up in the web of deceit and lies that we exhaust ourselves trying to break free. Step away from the web, and what do you see? You see a beautiful pattern of death all held up by two to three strands attached to something that a strong wind could destroy. Your job will be to find the two to three strands holding your web in place so that you can watch the web holding you back collapse. In doing this, you will be able to fly toward the light despite the darkness you are in.

Lastly, this book will drive the conversation forward about the true cost of your sins. In our current society and world, political correctness and fear of offending someone severely limit your ability to speak truth. This tactic, like most from the enemy, is a pre-packaged pattern. Find the strongest example of evil/hate for others and highlight that hate. If you can relate to the example in any way, apply the same feelings and disgust to what makes you feel uncomfortable and hinders your ability to speak truth. This has been going on for millennia, in case you think it is getting worse now.

However, this book will push straight through your feelings. Like Elijah said to Ahab in 1 Kings 18:18, "You have abandoned the Lord's commands and have followed the Baals. Now summon the people." I will be honest with you. Sometimes a man needs to be told he is a liar, cheat, narcissist, or a**hole. In the scripture above, Elijah went straight to the point. Here is what you did to get where you are right now, this is what is keeping you locked in your cycle, and here is how you can get out. This is one of the very reasons I enjoy reading the Bible. When I think about the boldness of some of these men and women, standing before a king speaking truth with love for a people, unafraid of offending, I become bolder myself. When you get as far down the rabbit hole of sin as I was, it takes someone who could honestly care less if I was offended to help me out. Tough love is still love when you provide it in a way that stands on truth.

Now—and I do mean now—this is not permission to just go around calling people names. This is not a pass to just call people out when you may only know one side of a story. I know many people who are quick to judge others but if you are judging based upon your own experiences, you are in the wrong and should keep your mouth shut. Nobody needs that in their lives whether you are right or wrong. I promise you that the way it will be received is not in love and will just further fuel the bomb that will eventually go off in their life.

I remember when I was still married, I had an affair. How is that for owning your mistake? Regardless, we decided to go to counseling. I remember the first counselor we went to. She came highly recommended, and I agreed to go. I sat there for an hour listening to how I was not a good man. My wife at the time had decided she was going to forgive me, and we were going to try and move forward. We went to the counselor for help, but we ended up worse than when we came in. The counselor's own experience, I later found out, and lack of unforgiveness for some things in her life found themselves in our counseling session. The result was another brick of guilt that went into my bag, further weighing me down, but I am getting ahead of myself. Pay attention to your surroundings, watch what you say if it implies guilt, and let your inner voice help you. Remember, you are your own worst enemy when highlighting someone else's mistakes.

WHY SHOULD I READ THIS BOOK?

By this point, I am sure that you have sought answers in prayer, counselors, and other books designed to help you obtain freedom and direction. Although each source has probably given you truths and challenges, none have spoken to you in a first-person account. I know exactly where you are. I know your thoughts, excuses, and struggles. I can empathize and sympathize with you as one who has been exactly where you are now. Sure, my situation may have been a little different, but the pattern is still the same. Remember, the enemy is still deploying the same tricks, using the same lies, and manipulating the same way since the beginning. Once you see the outcome of a choice you have made or are in the process of making from start to finish, I hope that you will change your mind. If you are not convinced to change, then just own who you really are. If you are okay with that, that is your truth and there is not much I can do for you. Only God can. Thus, this book is important and worth reading for the following reasons:

1) God does not want you to waste any more time living a life that is not yours; likewise, I will value your time. If

you are serious about becoming who you were created to be, you will read it.

I know it will be hard to find the time in-between Netflix, crammed social calendars, and the many lives you try to keep hidden. I want you to read this book even when you do not feel like reading. All I ask in return is for you to place yourself in the scenarios. You need to become the main character so that you can look around at your current situation. The similarities will be there whether you want to admit it or not, and in most cases, you will not. You may not want to admit them because you will be able to recognize the ending will be very similar to the scenario presented. I promise you that your being smarter, more pious, or more deserving will not change the outcome.

Movies are amazing. You have the ability to transport into another world for two to three hours. One of my favorite movies is *The Godfather*.[3] I could watch that movie over and over again despite knowing the ending. A funny thing happens when you know the ending of a movie; you notice the subtle details of a film. You notice things like veal is eaten before the famous shooting scene in the restaurant, that all the mob cars are black, or that when Vito was shot in the movie, oranges spilled to the ground. This event foreshadows the scene when he actually dies, as an orange is in his mouth while playing with his grandson. Despite knowing the ending, these details make the movie more realistic. Similarly, it is these details that will open your eyes to the true reality of the world created by your actions. I hope by "showing you behind the curtain," you will notice the small things that keep you playing the same part over and over again in your own

---
3 Francis Ford Coppola, The Godfather (March 24, 1972; Los Angeles, CA: Paramount Pictures).

movie. You will see that certain choices can truly only end in destruction and heartache.

When you read, please save your predictable comments, such as, "We love each other in a different way." I have no doubt. "She is everything my wife is not and just gets me." Yup. "She listens to me, and she knows my soul." Of course, she does. I hate to hit you with the truth, but patterns are foreseeable regardless of what you think. I will say one thing to you, and I want you to hear me well—I was the exception, too. Guess what else, the broke, suicidal guy I recently talked to, was also the exception.

2) I want to meet you where you are. I want to tell you stories through examples that you could truly see yourself in.

These examples are to help you see that even when you think you are in control, God's Words will always be true. The intellectual, prideful, do-it-myself side of me told me that I was in control, and I could make it work. The current version of me actually laughs in disgust thinking about my arrogance. Pay attention to how easily and subtly you can slide down a dangerous path. I need you to be slow to judge my choices and understand that it is easier playing Monday morning quarterback when you know the outcome of Sunday's game.

3) Judgment is a tricky thing.

At this point in your life, you most likely are judging those around you. Oh, you say you are not to everyone, and I think you actually believe that, but a closer look reveals something different. Judgment is the process of analyzing the world around you. We make a judgment every time we decide something is right or wrong, good or bad, should happen, or should not happen. These judgments objectively are classified as decisions. Everyone makes decisions daily. The problem lies in thinking you are somehow morally superior in deciding that something is wrong or right. When you assign your own emotions, past experiences, or cultural lens to a decision, that is where the judgment becomes negative. Those negative judgments are what will allow you to justify your actions since "you aren't as bad as that." A little hint going forward: if you find yourself saying "I'm not that bad," you're well on your way to being "that bad".

4) I want to motivate you to move from where you currently are and keep you from making the mistakes I made.

Motivation is what gives you a reason to act or behave in a specific way. Motivation can come in many forms, from achievement to the promise of adventure to increasing power. However, of all motivation forms, intrinsic motivation is by far the most powerful. Intrinsic motivation is the desire to obtain a goal that you have set for yourself. You are in control of your life. This simple statement is one I will repeat over and over again in the upcoming chapters.

In each and every person, there is a desire to be accepted, to discover our unique sense of purpose, and to succeed in what we have assigned as important. The degree of each "pull" of these desires is based upon an infinite number of factors, including genetics, trauma, life experiences, education, era of life, etc. However, despite these factors, your life is your own. You are responsible for your own happiness and nobody else. You are responsible for obtaining your peace and nobody else. You are responsible for your decisions and nobody else.

Moving forward and making decisions can be tough. I have seen Executive Officers unable to decide which woman to partner with but could run a multi-million-dollar company making hundreds of decisions a day, accurately and without hesitation. What causes this inability to decide? FOMO (fear of missing out), guilt, obligation, or expectation can be powerful influences on your inability to decide. We will dive deeper into this thought but know that your inability to decide leads to a loss of character, and the damage created in your tidal wave of indecision leaves a wake of destruction on your family, work creditability, and relationship with your Creator.

5) This book could change the trajectory of your life.

As I was moved to write this book, the purpose of the book was clear: Use your experiences to show the dark side of your decisions so it will educate and shine light on the thoughts or feelings that nobody discusses. It is this lack of conversation that keeps many in bondage to the illusions we create of what could be. If you truly step back and open your eyes, you will see many have done the same thing before you and many will do the same thing after you. There is a godly gift inside of you that when channeled outside of God's will creates bondage. Hope is wanting something to happen or be a reality. Godly hope is putting your trust in Him knowing a promise has been made and it will happen. On the flip side, if your hope is in yourself, thinking you know better and trying to force God's promises, then a price will be paid. That price starts as a lack of peace, then grows into fear, and ultimately into a disconnection from self and others. Now, not all hope outside of God is a bad thing. We can hope for a better job, a better future for our children, or for a sick relative to get better. The problem is not hope. The problem is, does that hope contradict the Word of God? If the answer is yes, then the hope you feel is the first step into the prison you will create for yourself. Once again, there is nobody to blame but yourself. You are in control of your life and when you change your trajectory and find true hope in your situation, the differences in your life will be obtained remarkably faster than you could ever realize.

WHO IS THIS BOOK FOR . . . YOU?

"You" are exactly what it implies. You, the reader, are my audience. It is likely that if you are reading this book on your own accord or if someone recommended it to you, you have made some poor decisions in life. You might not believe you have, but there is someone who thinks otherwise and that person maybe you. There is something different about you and, I promise you, that is something you can't hide. It is the quick temper, the hollow eyes, the increased stress, the unreliability, the silent and secret phones, the lack of motivation, the irritation at church, the isolation, the string of lies that begin and end without clear distinction, the weight gain or loss, the overall fatigue, the inability to make a clear decision, and the list goes on and on.

On the other side, you may be someone who has been living a life stuck in the middle. You may be the husband/wife, the best friend, son/daughter, father/mother, or church leader. This book will help you understand things that you may not be able to fathom. In doing this, I want you to know that you are not alone. The yelling, the lying, and the distance are all symptoms of poor decisions. One by one, a piece of the good-natured loving person that you used to know vanishes, but that does not mean gone forever. In reading this book, pay attention to the stories,

and ultimately, the downfall. Your job is to get educated and gain wisdom and understanding. Three things I want you to remember:
1) YOUR JOB IS NOT TO FIX THEM, even though you want to.
2) YOUR JOB IS NOT TO TOLERATE THEIR BEHAVIOR; you are not a martyr.
3) YOUR JOB IS NOT TO SACRIFICE YOURSELF; you are to make sure you let your true self out.

THIS BOOK IS YOUR TOUR GUIDE

This book hasten "Hard Lessons" that have been downloaded to me and each chapter will start with the verse that awoke my soul to move to the next lesson. I believe that God has delivered me from each scenario just for me to slip up again so that I can share my experiences, tragedies, and wins. As with all things in life, I am still a work in progress and will freely admit my mistakes. The façade of what others think is irrelevant to me, and the freedom I now experience has been elusive for a long time. I hope and pray that you will find a sense of freedom when you finish reading this book. I want you to truly evaluate your own life and choose to change its trajectory. I want you to succeed in your relationships and find your true purpose. I can assure you that living a life against God's will is NEVER the way, regardless of how much you have reasoned with yourself, taken verses out of context, or explained your story to others.

Second, this book is not linear. You may experience only one hard lesson and choose to turn back. You might need to experience all of them to truly find your way. The Bible contains stories of men and women who thought they knew better than God.

Some great individuals needed to experience lesson after lesson with each consequence becoming greater and greater. Remember that with each lesson, you will have a choice. This is your life and no one else's. So, with that said, the only person you can blame is yourself when it goes bad and, when you are finished, you won't be able to say, "I didn't know that would happen."

Third, this book needs to be read as a handbook, thesis, or tool. I am not making any doctrinal claims. I would like nothing more than to update the book for many editions as the conversation and realities of changed lives mount up. This book is just a small piece of God's arsenal to get you to live the life you were created for. I understand this will not apply to everyone, and that is a good thing.

> IF YOU ADMIT YOUR FAULTS, YOUR HABITS, AND YOUR STRUGGLES, I PROMISE YOU THAT WHAT YOU CAN LOSE IS NOTHING COMPARED TO LOSING YOURSELF.

Lastly, this book is designed to shine light on what you already know. The easiest thing to do is talk yourself into doing something or staying stuck in something when you know it is hindering you. It is okay to outgrow things. It is okay to transform yourself as you live life. We each have experiences that shape us into who we are. The question you have to ask yourself is, what am I transforming into? Am I losing my honor in the process? Am I losing those I love in the process? Am I being used to grow God's presence on Earth?

Be truthful to yourself where you are. I promise you there is someone more successful, sexier, younger, or possessing more intelligence than you. The truer with yourself you are, the more freedom you will find. If you admit your faults, your habits, and your struggles, I promise you that what you can lose is nothing compared to losing yourself. The fall of your character is more destructive than losing a marriage, relationship, or job. When your character is gone, you can't even start over properly until that is regained.

One last thought:: the number of names and judgments directed toward me, both warranted and not throughout my life, has truly astonished me. I have a feeling that you share this predicament. Yes, I am talking to you, "narcissist". What about your "psychopath"? Are you ready to read this book? How about the "master manipulator" in the back? Do you want to rise above the title given to you and become who God created you to be? Let this book challenge you, and when you find yourself laughing at my stupidity, stop and ask yourself, "Am I just as stupid?"

So, with that being said, it's time to start this journey into the dark, but I assure you that if you let the light in, you will find your way out regardless of how lost you are. Like losing weight, it took you years to get that dad bod. To expect it to disappear in weeks is laughable. One step at a time in the right direction and towards your purpose, and you will succeed. Best wishes and prayers as you proceed. You have been warned. . . .

HARD TRUTH #1:
IT WILL NOT AND CANNOT WORK.

"Do not be deceived: God cannot be mocked. A man reaps what he sows."
Galatians 6:7

Automobile accidents are a common occurrence. Of all accidents, human error accounts for 90 percent of them. A survey conducted in 2011 by Allstate Corp had some interesting findings. Of the participants surveyed, 64 percent of Americans rated themselves as "Excellent" or "Very Good" drivers. However, when these same drivers were asked to rate their friends on driving ability, their friends were considered "Excellent" or "Very Good" 29 percent of the time.[4] So wait, are you telling me that more than two-thirds of the general population believes they are amazing drivers and everyone else except for a few of their closest friends' suck? That is exactly what the research concludes. With this one study, an interesting revelation can be applied to other scenarios. People tend to exaggerate their

---

4 Allstate, New Allstate Survey Shows Americans Think They Are Great Drivers—Habits Tell a Different Story," Cision PR Newswire, 2 August 2011, https://www.prnewswire.com/news-releases/new-allstate-survey-shows-americans-think-they-are-great-drivers—-habits-tell-a-different-story-126563103.html.

abilities and think they are better than most in whatever they are doing. What does that sound like to you? Perhaps you think you know better than your friends, or even worse, God. Chances are you do not, and I hate to say it, but you are probably the one causing most of the accidents in this world amongst your church, families, or at work.

Like most people in this world, you know better than most everyone else. You sit on your throne of belief that you are somehow superior. This throne was constructed over time when a combination of experiences, success, positive reinforcement, and flattery eventually fed your pride long enough to overtake the humble spirit that also dwells within you. This pride is rampant amongst people and, unfortunately, pride comes before the downfall. If you think you can escape the downfall, think again.

Once upon a time, I met the most amazing woman. I remember the first time I saw her, and it seemed like time stood still. She was beautiful, successful, married, young, funny, attentive to my jokes, and sexual. She seemed to finish my sentences and I loved the feeling I had when I was around her. She made me come alive and seemed to understand me in a way that no other woman ever did. She was my destiny, my red thread, my heart's missing piece, the yin to my yang, or the peanut butter to my jelly. Whatever you chose to call it, one simple truth remained: she was another man's wife and God would never bless that nor condone this union. That which is not from God is from where??? You know the answer to this question, and you also know you are a better driver than most other people. (Insert sarcastic laugh.)

> **IF SHE IS MARRIED TO ANOTHER, YOU ARE MARRIED TO ANOTHER, OR YOU ARE BOTH MARRIED TO ANOTHER, YOU *DO NOT* HAVE NOR WILL YOU HAVE GOD'S BLESSING.**

I cannot tell you how many times I have heard similar stories. "She is my soulmate." "I never knew life until I met her." "We have been searching for one another and God determined we would be together." "My favorite food is steak and so is hers; look at all the similarities we have." Or my personal favorite, "fifteen years ago, we determined we were in the same city for a layover; it must be fate so I'm leaving my wife for this flight attendant." I cannot make this stuff up even if I tried. The crap we tell ourselves is truly shocking. Although these in the right context could be amazing, there is one detail you cannot forget. If she is married to another, you are married to another, or you are both married to another, you DO NOT have nor will you have God's blessing. My friend, without that, are you ready for the shit storm that you will face going forward? It is very real and unavoidable. Oh, that's right, you are a better driver and, of course, smarter. With all that pride, I hope you have great insurance, both auto and medical. Grab a mouthguard and helmet and get ready for the multiple crashes that are sure to follow. Oh, did I mention with each crash the stakes will get higher, and your insurance premium will continue to increase as you blatantly continue your recklessness? In the end, one day that premium will be so high that you will be unable to drive when the DMV suspends your license, as you can no longer be trusted to operate a vehicle.

Likewise, God will not be mocked. Marriage was created by Him. One day when you least expect it, God will suspend your ability to "drive" because He loves you and everyone around you. He does not want to see you cause any more damage. He wants you to come back to Him so He can make your life so much more peaceful. As Frank Sinatra said, "I DID IT MY WAY."[5] That may work for a short time, but I promise it will lead to ruin in one way or another. By the way, if you don't believe in God or His love for you, that's okay, because He believes in you.

I agree that you may have married the wrong person, not listening to God in the beginning, but if you are married now, He did not bring that "soulmate" into your life. God WILL NOT contradict Himself and would never purposely sacrifice one marriage for another. If you can find one scripture that says otherwise, I will gladly listen. I am not above admitting when I'm wrong. However, I have been doing this "I am amazing" life for so long that it will take a lot to convince me otherwise. Before you decide to call out my pride, understand that my decision is based on experience and time in the trenches. Just like with other things in life: Never tell a three-combat tour Marine infantryman that he does not know what war is like when you have been in the country for one week but feel you are qualified because you have read a lot of books and watched plenty of movies. That is called stupidity.

---

5 Frank Sinatra, vocalist, "My Way," Daniel Bedingfield, songwriter, March 1969, track 6 on My Way, Reprise.

DETERMINED TO MAKE THIS WORK

A strong will and resilience to overcome adversity are both a blessing and a curse. When channeled for an honorable purpose, mountains can move, and accomplishments can be achieved. However, when used for selfish pursuit, time is wasted and the body count of those you hurt can be substantial.

When I chose to cheat on my wife so many years ago, I had no idea the cost of my decision until years later. At that time, I had just gotten back from Iraq and felt entitled to get what I deserved. I was entitled to fulfill all my desires, and nobody was going to stop me. The pride I had was overwhelming, and I honestly believed I was not hurting anyone. I had seen people hurt and taken care of the wounded and thought I had this under control. I would live a life the way I wanted, and nobody would be the wiser. Boy was I wrong!

For context, let me remind you of something. War is destructive and vengeful and has been used to address conflicts amongst ideas, religions, and power since the fall of man. The cliché "War is Hell" is accurate. In every war, there is a winner and a loser. The definition of a win varies from less dead than the other guy to land gained. Likewise, in your own war over your sanity, there will be a winner, but at what cost? Are you willing to sacrifice your character, your purpose, your children, or your family to win? Another question, what does winning look like to you? The answers to these questions will determine the path you take from here on out. If you answer that you are willing to kill for your own self-interest, then I hope you do everyone around you a favor and go live life in a cave away from people. There is no need to destroy everyone around you. Be honest with yourself, and I hope one day, you find your way back. However, to the rest of you, look to create a cease-fire by finding peace with your mistakes, forgive yourself for your errors, and move forward in another direction.

The ability to move in another direction is courageous. Courage is doing something that you are fearful of regardless of the consequences. There is no doubt that you will most likely lose things but will gain something that nobody can take away from you—freedom of choice. By admitting your faults, you will no longer be bound to the fear of missing out on what you thought your best life would look like.

So, with this said, understand there will be a war within yourself over what you desire, what you need, and what you believe. They will not always line up and that is when you have to find the courage to move in a direction that maintains your character. Remember that some things are NEVER meant to work and continuing to put the square peg in the round hole will lead to nothing but wasted time. Oh, it may be fun for a while, but one day you will find yourself drooling in a white padded room you created for yourself, alone, and wondering what the hell happened. Determining to make a situation work destined to fail is a good way to grow older faster, turn your frustration into anger, and convert stability into unreliability.

THE ONE WHO UNLEASHED MY SINFUL NATURE

Stories begin in many different ways. One such way is, "to begin my life with the beginning of my life, I record that I was born." This beginning of Charles Dickens' *David Copperfield* implies that a life of truth exists all around us.[6] Another such way is, "Once upon a time . . ." which implies a fantasy story with an epic tale. Yet, another way is more direct, "The year was . . .", implying that the story will be anchored in fact. I will choose to start my stories in a way that will show you the snare that can trap anyone.

She was beautiful and I was prideful. Her smile had a way of radiating excitement inside of me and that was something I had not felt in a long time. She was so much different from my wife and that excitement turned into a want. A want is a tricky thing. It is very different from a need, but at the time I did not understand the difference. A want is something that you perceive will enhance the quality of your life. A need is something necessary to life.

I was tired. I was physically tired from one-hundred-hour work weeks. I was mentally tired from fighting my broken inner nature. I was spiritually tired from thinking I knew better than God. I was emotionally tired of feeling sad and unwanted. The combination of all four slowly lowered my defenses, and that is when it happened. I am going to wager that there are many of you who feel the same way. Understand this, when you feel this way, you have to own those feelings and cannot make excuses for it. Before the path becomes dark, ground yourself in truth and you can escape before the trap is sprung. I learned this lesson too late.

We worked together. I remember long nights, a mutual understanding of our work, and an avenue of escape from the mind-numbing days of our lives. Every day I would work, come home to sleep, and began to feel there was no support for my sacrifices at home. To this point, I was trying to be a good husband. I would work to provide for my family and sacrifice my health,

---
6 Charles Dickens, David Copperfield (London, England: Bradbury & Evans, 1850).

mental fortitude, and financial fruits to ensure all I was responsible for was taken care of. However, there was something very different with Abigail. We just connected.

It started as simple flirting. That escape was enough at first. However, just like everything else, we tend to push the boundaries further and further out as we cross one and then another. Each boundary gets crossed—not sprinting across them—but one step at a time. Likewise, the fall of your character happens slowly. It starts as an idea inside your mind. That idea then blossoms into fantasy. That fantasy births an escape from day-to-day life that can be far more appealing at times. When the kids are crying, the bank account never seems to increase, or your wife has a headache again, the mental escape is enough at first. It is a good "hit".

As time goes on, the "hit" must get bigger to have the same effect. When you don't deal with your current situation, what happens next becomes your reality. Your thoughts begin to betray you, and it happens. After about three months of flirting and tension building, we decided to meet outside of work. I knew what she wanted, and I felt the same. We needed that escape from life. Who would have known any different? We could meet intermittently and plan it accordingly. We found creative ways to talk while lying next to our spouses. At the time, Snapchat, WhatsApp, and other social apps had not yet been created. . . . you know those apps that have changed relationships forever. Instead, I would get out my iPad and pull up a word game similar to Scrabble. Oh, I would play her and others, but I utilized that chat room to its fullest potential. I think at one time I was actually playing games with my wife just to cover up my excessive playing time. It was through this game's chat capabilities that I was able to arrange meeting places and times around when the family would be home, most importantly.

Now, something happens during this transition from thought to reality. Truth becomes gray. You start to realize what is truly in your nature and the darkness that lies within your heart regardless of how pious you think you are. You will find and justify your actions by telling partial truths or answering questions very directly with no details. This is where you start hearing things such as, "You didn't ask me that, you asked me this," or, "I told you what I was doing, it just lasted longer," or, "I misjudged the time it began." I would find myself staying later at work so we could see one another, or I would take that extra lap around the block to get that last message in. The list of what I did would fill volumes of books, but I want you to see one very important thing. You have to see that reality and truth become blurred. Now, I do not plan to defend my thoughts with some philosophical debate. I know that some of you have justified your actions by quoting some dead writer or saying there are no absolute truths. You are free to believe what you want but if someone believes in unicorns, are they wrong if that is their truth?

The next step in the affair evolution was that seeing each other and communicating in secret was no longer exciting. The next "hit" must come, and this time, it comes faster and faster. Sex becomes a must so that you can connect spiritually, even though you think it is just an action. You think it is just a release from the reality of your world, but you will find that the reality of what you knew is also slowly fading. Your relationship with your kids becomes distant, your relationship with your spouse becomes annoying, and you look for more and more reasons to just get the hell out.

As it continues, sex becomes almost primal. The ten minutes here and there or the extended hour-long sessions truly become just an action. You justify the release because you deserve to be happy. You deserve this because you work hard. You deserve this because that's what you both want. Little did you know that the rabbit hole is getting deeper. You have created a relationship out of deceit and lies. You have cheapened both you and your partner. You have to understand that you have become addicted to the lies and dopamine release. You will look for any reason to keep it going. Likewise, you have turned your partner into a whore. She has to continue to live a life with you because you told her you loved her at some point. If she leaves you now, she was just a slut, and her conscious cannot handle that. She will give up everything for the illusion of your love and you will eventually resent her for that. There is no end to this regardless of how you think it will end. You tell yourself you can stop at any time. NOPE! It is quite unfortunate it has to be this way, but you cannot stop unless you are willing to make the hard decisions that will be necessary. The truth of your reality is nothing but a lie at this point. You will have to cut every string holding your life up and, honestly, be ready to move and just start over again.

So, I did just that. I moved my family hoping I could start over again. However, without confronting the addiction, lies, and deceit, my problems followed me and would have followed me to the opposite side of the world. I was now addicted to the rush and without confronting this addiction, I was destined to make the mistake again. I wish I could say that I learned my lesson and understood that it would never work out, but this would be a very short book. In addition, I would have regained six years of a fulfilling and honorable life, but it was not that easy. When you are stuck in a pattern of deceit, you cannot just walk away when you feel like it as there are usually someone else involved and they may have a different idea.

So just when I thought I had escaped the current situation, Abagail moved to my new city leaving behind everything for me. I eventually hated her for this decision but hated myself just as much—I was equally at fault. Here I was, looking to start over, but the dye had been cast. Little did I know, I had just primed the pump for the ability to do the same thing at the high-rollers table. The true nature inside of me had been released. I was smooth-talking, charismatic, and financially successful, and there were a lot of thirsty, hurting women. To my shame, I had lost my ability to distinguish truth from fiction. I enjoyed hedonism and the rushes it gave me. I would wake up void of emotion, but I would start the daily rounds of text messages, and that would give me my morning hits. As time went on, my marriage, my relationship with my kids was distant, and my thoughts would linger on peaceful days of my past. When I look back on my past, I can see one thing remained true: The relationships never worked because they were built on lies, and it took seven long years to finally learn that lesson.

Understand that you will not see your actions before they happen. You will constantly justify your actions and will talk with like-minded people, as it makes the poison go down so much easier. Every day, you have to decide whether you will be a good man or a bad man. Clinical Psychologist Jordan Peterson has said, "A harmless man is not a good man. A good man is a very dangerous man who has that under voluntary control."[7] When you have learned your own capabilities, own them, and set your footing on truth, you will finally understand what being a man is truly about, and God is looking for these men to stand watch for His people.

---

[7] Jordan Peterson, "A harmless man is not a good man. A good man is a very dangerous man, who has that under voluntary control," The Wisdom Warrior, https://thewisdomwarrior.com/2023/02/10/a-good-man-is-a-dangerous-man/.

HARD TRUTH #2:
RETAIN YOUR HONOR AND GOOD NAME AT ALL COSTS.
It May Be All You Have.

*"There is a way that seems right to a man,
but its end is the way to death."*
Proverbs 16:25 (ESV)

I want to ask you something. What is the most important thing in your life? Don't worry, I am not going to make you do some sort of fill-in-the-blank worksheet thing (that for some reason authors think we actually do). I am convinced that those blank lines are very important to increase the number of pages in the book to meet publisher standards. To anyone reading who likes to fill in the blank lines in a book, I salute you and all your overachiever-ness.

How about I take it a step further? What are you willing to sacrifice your life for? What did you think of? Was it a thought of yourself taking a bullet in some heroic fight to protect those you love? Perhaps, it is jumping in front of a car because your child went after a ball that rolled in the street and the driver was busy looking down at his phone? Sacrificing your actual body is an honorable way to die if protecting the innocent, but what I was thinking of was something entirely different. What are you willing to sacrifice for your next project at work that would potentially advance your career? How about, what are you willing to sacrifice for your mistress who knows exactly what you need? Let's take it even deeper, what are you willing to sacrifice for your honor or integrity? The answer to these questions depends on what you believe and what is most valuable to you. In a simple sentence, what is most important in your life, and what are you willing to sacrifice to protect it?

Now, follow along with me and I will bring it all together, but I must lay some foundation for my particular choice of words. When I was a kid growing up in New Jersey, I used to hear the word "respect" thrown out left and right. I was told I had to respect my parents. I was told I had to respect my teachers. I was told I had to respect anyone who was older or had a position of authority. Although the principal purpose of this was for a good reason, the term respect was confusing. When someone has respect for you, it means they find value or worth in you. Respect is not "I have to agree with you or follow you blindly." Notice the difference—to disagree with someone or how they behave is perfectly acceptable. However, what is not okay is disagreeing and thinking that person has no value. The importance of respect is displayed in the Bible as it is mentioned thirty-four times. To simplify this word, it is how you see someone in the world.

Likewise, honor is a word that can be used loosely without truly understanding. Honor to some is not important because of how a person views the world. Honor is defined as showing esteem for one deserving of respect. What this means is that honor is the way the world sees you. If you live a life for yourself, then honor is a nuisance to your self-absorbed life. However, there is one problem—honor is used 147 times in the Bible. With a word being used that frequently, it must be important and should not be ignored. Remember God will not be mocked. To live a life without honor not only sets you up for a useless existence but ensures you will struggle constantly as God wants to help you regain that honor so you can be used for His purpose.

> WHEN YOU ACHIEVE THE ABILITY TO MAINTAIN YOUR HONOR AND VIEW OTHERS WITH RESPECT, THEN YOU WILL REGAIN YOUR INTEGRITY AND WHO YOU ARE AS A MAN.

With that said, let's create a simple formula:
Respect + Honor = Integrity
How you see the world + How the world sees you =
How God sees you

Integrity is your name or the condition or quality of being complete or undivided. Do you like being called a womanizer? Do you like "a**hole"? Do you like being a selfish prick? Somewhere along the way, your respect for others or honor got skewed. When you achieve the ability to maintain your honor and view others with respect, then you will regain your integrity and who you are as a man. This is the most important thing to find if you are lost in this world and the most important thing to keep if you have it. Remember, you must keep your good name regardless of the cost to remain whole for your family, job, and calling.

Let me be the first to say that maintaining your integrity may mean making hard choices. It may mean leaving a job earning six figures. It may mean leaving the best sex you ever had. It may mean leaving that lake house for a kiddie pool in your backyard. The price you may have to pay can sometimes be more than you are willing to sacrifice. I know, I've been there. Words such as honor were what the movies portrayed it as. As long as I was providing for my family, I was doing the honorable thing. I did not understand that honor was the way the world saw me. I did not realize that my choices to bend the truth, live a life thinking I was entitled to more than I had, and fulfill sexual desires had sacrificed my honor and, as per the equation, my integrity.

Now, I wasn't an idiot. I knew exactly what I was doing but like most, I had it under control. I knew that if anyone found out what I was doing, they may talk behind my back or make gestures to display their distaste for me. Who honestly cares about that? Remember, society today talks about living for yourself and not caring what anyone thinks about you. Seriously, this is what is taught, and I bought that hook, line, and sinker. What they don't teach you is the consequences of a life for yourself. Sayings like YOLO (you only live once) or FOMO (fear of missing out) can be found on any YouTube channel or social media account. It has become a rampant slogan for people to dissociate from society as a whole and quite honestly, numbing or dulling out your responsibility to those around you. Although the sayings have merit, the context to use them MUST be applied to a life that works with the purpose of your creation. It must be placed in a sentence that compliments who you are for the Kingdom and not just to please you.

I am not some martyr. I still will have a drink and I like sex. I would 100 percent revert back to that life if I was unaware of the consequences. However, I have seen what happens when I live a life for me. I have seen the price to be paid and there is no escaping it. Oh, I know you think you will not have to pay, but that is just pure bullshit. I would suggest trying to figure it out now as the price will get steeper with each passing day until one day, your butcher's bill will come due. Someone will have to pay it for you and on that day, may God forgive you.

Remember my words when you are the dishonest shitbag father in your hometown. Remember my words when you can't post on social media since a lie may be revealed. Remember my words when you are bankrupt and in debt so high that Dave Ramsey will call you "Stupid". Remember my words when your kids refuse to see you and you are all alone on Christmas Day watching reruns of the James Bond marathon on TNT. THE PRICE MUST BE PAID but still, for some, that will not be enough to shake them. My advice: don't give up your integrity at all costs. The price and time needed to regain it cost more than the lost time spent living without it.

DANGEROUS SLOPE

Iniquity is a word that those in Christian circles may or may not understand. Iniquities are those hidden, festering, insidious flaws inside each and every one of us. Most of us do not have to look very far or can catch a glimpse of our inequities by looking at our fathers' family tree. If Dad was a womanizer, guess what, you have that in you. If Granddad was corrupt in business, guess what, you may be corrupt in business. By evaluating where we come from, we can usually gain insight into where we could go. This knowledge is important not only for you but for your children and your children's children. A line in the sand must be drawn. Are you willing to confront your ancestors and all that made your family name? Only you can make that choice . . .

Each generation will have the opportunity to face family iniquities. The iniquity that you will have to face could be one or many. Although a person may not know that one exists, search your heart for the pull you have towards something. Do you feel drawn to always having the last word in an argument? Do you feel the need to validate yourself by appearing more important than you actually are? Do you feel the need to seek affirmation in a good morning text by a man or woman? These in themselves do not mean you have done something wrong, but they may reveal certain generational flaws in your DNA. (For all you science folks, this is not a book on DNA nature. I understand that choices do not live in DNA. Follow along and don't get sidetracked.)

Each day, I understand that we all make choices. Those choices reflect who we are and what we believe. Not all iniquities will ruin lives but the choices you make will dictate if it releases within you or skips you. What if I told you that the choices you make are similar to the ones your grandfather made? If you knew the iniquity in your family line, what would you do about it? I will tell you what I did about it—nothing—and that nothingness revealed just what I had lost. However, it wasn't until years later that I understood the true gravity of that decision.

My grandmother, my father's mother, lived to one hundred years. She was a kind, loving, woman who truly saw the good in those around her. I loved her and learned what a servant's heart truly looked like, but little did I know, she held an important piece of information that would forever give me an understanding of who I was and what I was capable of. At the time of her hundredth birthday, I was deep in "the shit" as I like to call it. "The shit" is when you find yourself going around in circles. You don't know what is coming at you and from what direction. You wake up to look at your phone, to see who found out about the night before while you were sleeping. Did you cover your tracks well enough to not be found out, or did you leave a parking stub in your car from where you were the night before (true story)? Did the spa you were taking your girlfriend to call to confirm your appointment the day before using the number of the other girl you took there, as it was her number on file (true story)? Did your teenage daughter post a TikTok on her page showing her at her house the night she was supposed to be with you (also true)? Like I said, "the shit" is never knowing what the next day will bring but not in a peaceful, joyful way. Back to the story...

One day I went and visited my grandmother as she was not doing well and dying. I remember sitting down in the chair across from her. She looked at me and said, "Have you finished with my best friend?" I looked at her and said, "I am your grandson." She said, "no you aren't. My grandson is a good boy. You are my husband, George, and my son, George." At first, I did not understand that, but as she regained an awareness of what was around her, I began to understand when she told me more. She told me that she found her husband, my grandfather, in bed with her best friend shortly after they were married. My uncle followed and cheated on his wife. I asked her why nobody ever told these stories, and she said she was afraid to bring shame to the family. At that moment, I realized I had become my family. I was a product of generational flaws, and I did nothing at that time. Why did I do nothing? I had lost my honor, and even more importantly, my integrity. The strength to stand up, fight for my family, and break the cycle was not even a thought.

Funny things begin to happen when you lose honor and integrity. Someone can show you your exact flaw and you still can't see it. This is the classic Monty Python scene of the duel of the black knight. "Your arm is off. No, it isn't. It's just a flesh wound."[8] We laugh at that scene, but it really is the truth. You have to do all you can to maintain your honor and integrity before you can see the truth right before your eyes. I promise you it is not just a flesh wound. It is the hearts of your wife and children, sacrificed on your altar of hedonism. You are such a good dad hiding the truth instead of confronting it. You are such a good father teaching your children to seek their own selfish desires. Father of the Year goes to this guy . . . powerhouse in the office and shithouse at home. So, I ask, what would you do? Are you where I was, or do you still have the fight in you? If you have the fight in you, hold on to that and do not slip further. If you do not, maybe another story will help you find your way back.

---

8   Terry Gilliam and Terry Jones, Monty Python and the Holy Grail (April 3, 1975; London, England: Python (Monty) Pictures), screenplay.

"I WOULD DO ANYTHING FOR MY KIDS"

My family was living in South Carolina when my first affair started. I had just relocated from North Carolina and had been home from Iraq for six months. I was headstrong, prideful, felt entitled, and had a wife who refused to have sex with me. Before I continue, you need to understand a few things. First, I am not justifying my actions for what I did. At the time, I felt owed more than what I was getting. Second, I was unaware of the iniquities within me, just waiting for the catalyst to get out. Third, I never stopped to ask what I was not providing to my wife and why. Lastly, I lived in the moment and was not able to think of the consequences of my choice. I needed sex. I felt entitled to getting sex, and if my wife was not going to give it to me, I was going to find it elsewhere. Every night, I would put the women and children to bed and go looking for dinner. I had an urge although it was very misguided. I fell into society's traps, and I was going to fulfill it.

By this point in my marriage, there was not much left. We did not care to make one another happy. I would work constantly, in my mind trying to support my family, but I have come to suspect it was an outlet to escape life. My wife stopped trying to love me and even said to me at one time, "I wish you would go have sex with a nurse so that I can just divorce you. I will even pick her out for you." At this point, adultery had not occurred so there were no grounds for divorce in a Christian marriage as is believed, but it was becoming a game of willpower. I would flirt, watch whatever I pleased, drink whatever I wanted, and come home whenever I chose. How long could I last before breaking? We all have a breaking point regardless of how strong our will is, how strong our faith is, or how strong our desire is to do what we think is right.

What you have to understand is that at this time in my life, I did not fail at things because that would have shown the world that I had flaws. That was unthinkable. I would never admit to the world I was wrong or there was something wrong with me. I had to stay camouflaged among the picture I had painted to the world. I enjoyed the attention and envy from others. I enjoyed having the trophy wife whom others undressed with their eyes. I would never have admitted anything differently. My pride choked out any semblance of a relationship with God, let alone anyone. Do you really think I was going to admit my marriage was over in my current state of reckless, hedonistic living?

I am just going to chuckle now because I know my audience. You will not admit that either. It's okay, I know what you are not admitting to. Yes, I am talking to you, owner of the Chick-fil-A down the street. How about you, megachurch assistant pastor? Is your intrapersonal life one big charade? "I will lose my ability to work if I reveal my truths." "My future dreams will never come true if I tell those around me my desires and thoughts." Believe me when I say, I understand completely so this is what makes it hard. You have to keep people believing in one thing while you live out something else. While you live out your ruse (a cunning attempt to trick someone), I want you to remember that leaving your wife before starting down an adulterous path can save your honor and integrity if you truly have a hardened heart. If you do not and keep thinking no one will find out, you are very, very wrong and your lost integrity along the way will ruin you more than it would if you just left your wife. The stain of your choices will haunt you in more ways than you can imagine and may even force you to write a book just so others do not fall down the same path.

Now, a hardened heart happens when there is a serious breach of the marital bond—a serious trust breakdown—and there is no true repentance or willingness to look at the issues and how that's affected the marriage. Matthew 19:8 writes, "Moses permitted you to divorce your wives because your hearts were hard. But it was not this way from the beginning." This is important because I believe marriages stay together for the wrong reasons. In particular, Christian marriages tend to stay connected when there is no provable adultery regardless of the condition of the heart. Some of these marriages are so toxic that some people actually cheer for a breakup. These are hardened hearts, and they affect all, especially the children.

I feel I have to give a disclaimer. I do not advocate for divorce. I believe in the sanctity of marriage, that each partner was brought into the other's lives to help one another succeed in whatever calling God has placed upon them. I do not believe that your partner is necessary for you to achieve success, but they can help you navigate your success. The right partner can make life more enjoyable while refining you into a better version of yourself. However, I believe that abusive, co-dependent, fearful marriages are a sign of hardened hearts, and to fall on your sword as a martyr in these conditions just makes you an idiot. Likewise, if you are full of pride, you have lustful desires that you cannot control, you are constantly looking around at what you don't have, or you believe the grass is greener in the next field over, it is time to evaluate your heart. If you have no desire to change that, then make the choice to maintain your integrity, leave your wife, and quite possibly your kids for a short time until you get things figured out, and try to disregard what others say about you. Thank me later for unwasted time in the future when you finally decide enough is enough.

My children mean the world to me, and I suspect yours do, too. The thought of not seeing them was something I could not comprehend, and I was not going to entertain that. I had a good relationship with them, and I was not going to change that. What I did not understand was that my decaying heart was leading to the destruction of our relationship for years to come. I remember my wife telling me that if I divorced her, she would take the kids to Virginia, and I would see them for holidays and weekends when I could. I was in the military, and that was our home of record. There was nothing I could do to stop them. They were going to be eight hours away and I did not have schedule flexibility to sustain a relationship with them. I still had a year left before I paid my obligation, and the decision I made still haunts me to this day. My heart was hard toward my wife; I felt owed more than what I had, but I did not want to not see my kids. So, I chose to start an affair that led to lies, deceit, and heartache. I decided I would take the chance that nobody would find out and keep a relationship with my children. In a nutshell, I chose to dishonor myself and lost my integrity. This decision led to seven years of endless cycles of lost trust and my having to repair my relationship with them. Looking back, if I chose to leave for that year, maintain my integrity, and then restart my relationship with them, we all would have been better off, and perhaps, the sins of the father would have stopped there. They would not have seen me become what I did over those seven years with lost honor and would have saved hours repairing the damage done. Believe me when I tell you, the price paid for my choice is something I would not wish on anyone. For endless days, they did not want to see me. They didn't want anything from me. I sacrificed my kids' childhood, forcing them to grow up quickly and without true guidance from a father. The thought still sickens me, and I hope you do not fall victim to this pain.

As I started this chapter, I was reminded of Proverbs 14:12 that there is a way that seems right to a man, but in the end, it leads to death. Death can be a physical, emotional, or spiritual. Likewise, death may come upon those you are charged to protect and provide for. If you are reading this book, think about the costs of your decisions. Stories of shattered relationships litter the ground around you. Choose to maintain your honor and integrity and do whatever it takes. It is okay to not see your kids—for a time. God will forgive you if you truly repent, and guess what, your kids will, too. The time it takes to get there is just a lot longer when you fall. God will work in you to repair relationships, but only if you are a man of integrity in His eyes. When that is lost, you will have to regain that before you can fix the broken. Webs of lies, financial ruin, and fear of losing what your body tells you it wants make it very, very hard to restore what you lose. This fight for your integrity is so hard that many never regain it. However, it is one you should not have to face to begin with. Integrity is the most important thing in your life. It is the cornerstone of all relationships, business deals, and purpose for your creation. DO NOT LOSE IT!

HARD TRUTH #3
GUILT CAN MAKE YOU DO BAD THINGS.

"As a dog returns to its vomit, so fools repeat their folly."
Proverbs 26:11

Throughout my life, I have made many choices. At the time of this writing, I am forty-four years old. It is agreed upon through research that the average person makes 35,000 choices a day. When I crunch the numbers, I realize that is 12,775,000 a year. In my lifetime alone, I have made approximately 562,100,000 choices!!! Now last I checked I am not perfect, so it is safe to say that not all my choices are the right ones. Even if I have made the right choice 99.99% of the time, I have made 562,100 bad choices. Let that sink in for just a moment.

Now, I will freely admit that some bad choices might just be mismatching the color of your shoes or eating that extra Taco Bell burrito. These choices have little consequences in the grand plan of your life. However, even if 99.99% of those bad choices are trivial, that leaves 562 bad choices that can affect the outcome of my life. When you actually stop and think about this, you are destined to make bad choices about something major in your life. There is no escaping that outcome despite every attempt to live a "good" life.

> **WHEN YOU KNOW THAT A BAD CHOICE HAS BEEN MADE, WHAT STARTS AS A CONVICTION FROM THE HOLY SPIRIT CAN TURN INTO SOMETHING EVEN MORE SINISTER.**

As we make that bad choice, you must understand that God already knows the choice you have made is a bad one, and yet He still loves you. He wants you to repent and move forward in life but for some of us, that choice is not easily made. See, there is something that keeps you from accepting His freely given grace and this is continuously reaffirmed to you by those you hurt, those you cheated, and those who do not suffer from the inequities found within you. When you know that a bad choice has been made, what starts as a conviction from the Holy Spirit can turn into something even more sinister. You begin to believe that you must pay a price for your bad decision and that you must constantly suffer. Over time, despite your best efforts, you begin to believe this to be true. Your very character and essence begin to change and ultimately the condition of guilt takes hold and paralyzes you from real repentance and seeking atonement for your decision. Guilt is the condition, not feeling, that you have done something wrong and, my friends, a condition just doesn't go away until you face it and the consequences of the choice.

Guilt is defined as responsibility for having done something wrong or the state of one who has committed an offense. You will notice that feeling is not mentioned in the definition. A feeling is a street sign for your life. It tells you that you are going the wrong way, speeding, or that you should stop and look both ways before moving forward. Guilt is much more, and I believe this is what can keep people in bondage to their sins of the past.

On the other hand, conviction is sent from the Holy Spirit when you have sinned. When you are on the wrong path or making the wrong choices, conviction allows you to turn back or alter the path you have chosen. Conviction will last as long as you stay unrepentant, but at the same time, can help restore your relationship with God. On the other hand, guilt can last a lifetime, all the while making us ineffective and miserable. We must understand the difference so we can break free from our sinful behavior that can lead to bad choices.

HOW GUILT ENTERS YOU

In my research, experience, and observations, I have concluded that guilt is one of the great poisons of life. It turns strong men weak and gives power to others over your life. It is a tranquilizing dart that keeps you alive but forces you to drool over yourself helplessly to fight back. It is no wonder why many of us are affected by it.

The process of suffering from guilt enters us through an opening we have created in our minds. The opening usually comes in the form of doubting our true calling in life, drifting with no purpose, or believing we deserve something that is not given to us. This is another way of saying that we doubt our value, we have not accepted our position of authority over our lives, or we have an exaggerated sense of entitlement that allows us to take what is—clearly—not ours to have. These openings in themselves will not bring guilt, but they do sit idly waiting for a sin to attach themselves to and then begin their work on your mind.

Never knowing when you will mess up, once sin enters into your life, the opening turns into a door with a blinking light, GUILT ME!! I DESERVE IT FOR WHAT I HAVE DONE! for the world to see. By not understanding your power over your life, you allow others to start dictating what you are supposed to feel and how you are supposed to think about yourself, and you will believe you must have something seriously wrong inside that caused you to commit the sin you did. If you begin to believe that you must be living a false life, then the pain cuts even deeper and the cycle of guilt will begin.

I remember when my wife and I formally separated. I left the house for a weekend as she was moving out. I came home and I was shocked. I kid you not, she left me my clothes, the guest room bed, a few things that she could not dispute were mine, one plate, one fork, one bowl, one spoon, one cup, and one knife. Attached to the bed was a note that said, "You are all alone and you deserve it." At that moment, the actions of my sin came crashing down over me and I gave up my authority over my life and believed what she had just said. It pierced straight through my soul. Oh, I did deserve what had happened but that was not for her to decide. At that moment, that simple letter changed my path for years to come. The burden of guilt came flooding over me and the condition overtook me.

Now, there is a difference between deserving the consequence of your sin and guilt. The consequences of my sin would have dictated that I brought it all upon myself and agreed that my wife did the right thing. She had left me to think about my choices in life and all that I had built with her was gone. The problem with that was that I allowed her to become my judge. I gave her authority over my thoughts and emotions. That was a mistake, and I could not see it at the time. I was guilty of a sin, the price had been paid, and it was time to turn around and rebuild my life from the ashes. However, she told me what I was supposed to believe about myself in that moment and how I deserved to live my life knowing I had destroyed my family.

I know that many others will relate to this story. I remember many years ago, I spoke with a man who had an affair. He had confessed his affair to his wife. He tried to maintain his integrity despite his mistakes and for that, I praise him. However, guilt had settled in deep within him. Despite his transparency and her supposed forgiveness, she created a podcast that was designed to help women who have suffered the same thing. I believe that God uses sin and tribulations to further His Kingdom and from what I have heard, the podcast was a success. The problem was that as she became greater, he became weaker. The burden of what he had done became heavier with each and every episode. See, he was told that to make up for what he did to her, he had to listen to her podcasts. He was forced to constantly relive the sin in a public forum and not from a position of authority. He had let someone else dictate what he was supposed to feel and believe. He gave someone else authority over his life and guilt overtook him. He was struggling to heal from his sin. There was no way in his current state that he could use his journey to help others. He was stuck in a pattern of despair with no way to break free because he was told he deserved what was happening, and he agreed. Can you see the pattern? When you let others tell you what you deserve, that is when guilt enters.

Advice: Stop allowing others to judge you. God is your judge. Let His convictions guide you to true repentance or prepare to live with the weight of guilt dragging you down and forcing you to repeat the same mistakes because you are not worthy of a different life.

HOW GUILT AFFECTS YOU

In my profession, people will routinely ask me, "What are the side effects of this medication?" My response is usually, "I have no idea what they could be for you until you take them." If there is a "black box" warning, I make sure to warn folks, but to go through hundreds of side effects will only cause anxiety. Otherwise, I have no idea how your body will respond to any given medication, hence why drug commercials list literally everything as a potential side effect. The body responds in weird ways to certain things, and sometimes the reaction may be life-threatening. With that said, how might guilt affect you? Guess what, I have no idea. I can give you the black box warnings but otherwise, the side effects will not be known unless you experience it, and let's hope that day never comes.

When I think about guilt, I am reminded of a box office failure that truly displays and captures an array of emotions and the consequences of your actions. More than that, *The Shawshank Redemption*[9] is an insightful movie about guilt. Many characters handle guilt in various ways in the movie. Remember, this is a condition. This is more than a feeling or awareness of a sin.

The story begins with a guilty verdict of a man convicted of murdering his wife and her lover. The man is sentenced to two consecutive life sentences and from his arrival at Shawshank, the story truly begins. The innocent man, Andy, believes that his drinking and what happened to his wife was essentially his fault. In fact, in the movie, Andy says, "I killed her, Red. I didn't pull the trigger, but I drove her away. And that's why she died. Because of me. The way I am." He believed that he deserved his incarceration and all the things that happened to him during those eighteen years in prison. Andy doubted his value and his purpose in life. However, with the help of his best friend, Andy finally discovered the path to freedom from guilt—to help others in their situations. When Andy realized his true calling and took it beyond what the walls of Shawshank provided, that is when he finally escaped the prison. It took him eighteen years to break free from his guilt. All those around him confirmed his belief that he deserved all that happened to him, and it was when he finally stopped believing them that true freedom arrived.

On the other hand, Red is truly guilty of murder, but he befriends Andy, and together, they begin a journey of redemption. As the name of the movie implies, I believe redemption comes from the condition of guilt both externally (societal guilt) and internally (condition of guilt). Nevertheless, Red's guilt entered when he felt he deserved his punishment, but he never accepted

---

9 Frank Darabont, The Shawshank Redemption (October 14, 1994; Burbank, CA: Warner Bros. Entertainment Inc.).

responsibility for his actions. He never accepted responsibility for his life and thus we see him drifting with no real purpose. Red was ineffective, never bettering himself, since he believed he belonged exactly where he was. For forty years, Red lived with the guilt of his sin. Towards the end, and I believe with the help of Andy, Red finally accepts responsibility for his actions and finally takes authority over his younger self. By doing this, he steps into a position of authority. In fact, he held himself in so much authority, that he did not even care what the parole board thought. He was a man free from guilt, and that is when his bondage was broken. Red became a free man.

Lastly, Warden Samuel Norton had an exaggerated sense of entitlement. He believed he deserved something he didn't have and would torture prisoners, embezzle money, and participate in conspiracy to murder and many more crimes to feed his entitlement. Each day he would suppress his guilt with more and more sin. He would continue to do the same thing over and over again. Now, I have no idea of whether he was tormented by his decisions, but in the end, he succumbed to guilt. His guilt and pride became so heavy that the picture he uses to hide his sins from the world says it all, "His judgment cometh and that right soon." Samuel put a gun to his head and pulled the trigger.

The side effects of guilt are unpredictable. Some will try to help others while putting on a façade to the world that everything is okay. When they believe they deserve exactly what they are receiving, they will remain stuck until they understand their value. Others will drift through life with no real purpose. They will blame others for their problems and will serve no real value to themselves or others around them. Until they accept responsibility or step into a position of authority over their lives, they will remain unimpactful. Still, others will continue the same behavior over and over and over again. There is guilt inside, but they have no desire to stop. They feel they will overcome it themselves and their inflated egos will keep them returning to their vomit and repeating the cycle. This cycle will continue until they have hit rock bottom, have a true "come to Jesus moment", or worse, end it all so as not to deal with the burden of the guilt anymore.

THREE PROPERTIES OF GUILT

Guilt has to be dealt with. The condition of unresolved guilt can destroy your life and the effects can be dire to all around you. Another condition that can show the same pattern is depression. I could devote an entire book to depression, but I will only say a few words. Depression is a mental health condition. It affects people in ways that we still do not completely understand. I am not a psychiatrist or therapist, but I do understand the effects on the body and on those around you. The condition of guilt is very similar.

Guilt lingers and can be passed down to the next generation.

Guilt carries consequences when not accurately diagnosed and treated.

Guilt will dictate certain decisions that will leave the unafflicted person scratching their head as to why.

As I have discussed in a previous chapter, it should not be so hard to understand that things pass from generation to generation. When guilt enters a person, there is a very real chance the children of that person will suffer the same fate. Whether guilt manifests or not, it is wrapped in multiple variables. Children will display guilt usually when they do not understand their value or feel they have no authority over their lives. The first time I saw this, I was sitting at dinner with my daughter. I noticed that she was really quiet. I asked her what the problem was, and she told me that she was responsible for me not living with her mom anymore. What started as a misunderstanding developed into complete guilt. She did not understand her value and felt helpless to change the situation. For her to feel sadness, anger, or a myriad of other emotions would be perfectly normal. However, in this situation, a condition of guilt overtook her. I realized that I had passed a condition of guilt onto her. Her guilt was not from her mistakes but from mine. I allowed her to feel less valuable than she is and recognized that my condition started her down a path that we are (finally) pulling out of. No choice you make is without consequences. What a sobering reminder. Sometimes those consequences cannot be seen until much later and reveal themselves in those you love.

> **WE MUST CHANGE THE WAY WE VIEW GUILT AND UNDERSTAND THAT IT IS TRULY A CONDITION OF THE MIND.**

Likewise, the consequences of guilt will keep you repeating the same mistakes if you have no idea what you are dealing with. As a physician, what I examine and test will help me diagnose a condition to treat it correctly. However, there is a saying in medicine, "If you don't know it exists, you will never diagnose it." I believe this is true of guilt. We must change the way we view guilt and understand that it is truly a condition of the mind. Those who are reading this understand that there is no excuse for some of your actions despite being in a state of guilt. I promise you that a person operating in a condition of guilt knows exactly what they are doing. The problem is they feel helpless as if they have no control. They most likely do not understand that guilt is an illness that controls you and buries deep within your soul.

Lastly, guilt has ruined more relationships than I can count. I have made decisions that I look back and say, WTF! I met many amazing people over the years but where are they now? I squandered many of the relationships I have entered in the past. I allowed my children to become attached to women and friends who are no longer in my life. Many times, I would choose to return to my vomit and sacrifice those healthier relationships on the altar of deception. The guilt I felt over the choices I made disrupted my ability to have an honest relationship. I would continue to fall back into patterns of not knowing my true purpose or finding the strength to take control of my life. I remember my mom telling me once, "I would never let my friend's daughters date you. I may lose a friend before it is all over with the dumbass decisions you make." That was a hard one to hear but like the rest of the moments that led to my release from guilt, this seed yielded some incredible fruit.

FREEDOM FROM GUILT

I told you in the beginning that I am not a pastor, apostle, or teacher. I will not throw verse after verse at you; however, this Word began to silence the voices around me, brought me to a place of repentance, and set me free from guilt. We each have a journey to come back to who we were before, and it was this verse that began to transform me. I believe that it might illuminate what some of you have been missing.

David had impregnated another man's wife. He had tried to cover up the act by lying, manipulating, and ultimately having the husband killed to keep from having to face the consequences. David, the man after God's own heart, who most likely made 99.999% good choices, had made a really bad one. After the consequences for his bad choice had come full circle, David finally realized the true nature of guilt and in Psalm 32, he described exactly what we all feel when guilt overtakes us and how to escape its grasp over our life.

> *When I kept silent, my bones wasted away through my groaning all day long. For day and night your hand was heavy upon me; my strength was sapped as in the heat of summer. Then I acknowledged my sin to you and did not cover up my iniquity. I said, "I will confess my transgressions to the Lord" and you forgave the guilt of my sin. Therefore let all the faithful pray to you.— Psalm 32:3-5*

What David just said in twenty-first century language is this:

I am really freakin' tired. My hair is turning grey. I am out of shape and my belly is getting bigger. My family and friends think I've gone crazy, but I refuse to make changes because I am exhausted each and every day. I am tired of the lies, the manipulation, and I am stuck in this cycle of pain that I feel I may deserve. However, I have hit a point in my life where I have finally found some strength to change my patterns. God, I know I have sinned against you and others consciously. I knew what the right thing was to do and did the exact opposite. I have come to realize that there are deep things inside of me passed down from my parents and their parents before that predispose me to certain sins, but this is no excuse. So, with all I have learned, felt, and understand, I confess that I have intentionally disobeyed what I know to be true. I have hurt others around me and have allowed them to keep me locked into bondage, having to constantly repeat the sin over and over again because I felt I deserved it. My spirit has diminished under this weight of burden, and You have finally set me free. I will pray for those I have hurt and hope they find forgiveness in prayer to you. With passion spoken (Selah).

HARD TRUTH #4
HOLIDAYS SUCK...

"I will repay you for the years the locust have eaten."
Joel 2:25

At this point in the book, I am just going to meet you where you are. I am going to be blunt without concern for the repercussions of my words. If you have strayed very far from the path you should be on, if you are juggling two women, or if you are manipulative or carrying around guilt, holidays just flat-out suck. Christmas time is just one big Yule Time Log of Crap, and all other holidays can keep their Happy: New Year's, Valentine's Day, Birthday, and Thanksgiving festivities to themselves. They stress me out.

Before I am completely dragged over burning hot coals, the context for this chapter comes from the eyes of a selfish individual. This individual is confused about decisions made or not made, confused about why he feels the way he does, or confused about his purpose in this life. However, I want to make it clear that I will not be downplaying certain documented correlations with holidays and increased mental health struggles and suicide. Times of celebration can be very stressful for certain people.

Holidays can feel like days of unrealistic expectations for people suffering from depression, sadness over loss, or anxiety about having to deal with family dysfunction. This is tragic, and we must remember that everyone has a story or something they are dealing with. However, a certain group of individuals hate holidays for extremely selfish reasons. These people are schemers, and during the holidays, things can get interesting. Manipulators have a rough time with holidays It is that time of year when lies have to be perfect. They have to be able to justify their absence from certain things. They have to create and devise new patterns or ways of doing things to not draw suspicion. This gets extremely difficult and extremely exhausting. So, like I said, holidays suck.

HOLIDAY OF DECEPTION

As a kid, I loved holidays. They were magical, as I did not have school, and on almost every holiday, I received presents that I had seen on TV over and over on Saturday mornings. As a family, we got to eat off the fancy dishes and, of course, sit in the room my sisters and I were never allowed to go into. As you can imagine and may have experienced yourself, this was very exciting for an eight-year-old. However, life moves on and as we mature into adulthood, we are left with memories of a simpler time in our lives. For most, these memories help drive our continued love for a holiday, and the ability to take a break from the world without judgment can also contribute to our excitement. Holidays are a time we can unplug and spend time with those people who are important in our lives. However, what happens when you have been telling two people that they are just as important to you? What does the holiday look like then?

The story I want to tell will help shine some light on what happens when you are living a life that is built upon lies and can only exist in a world of manipulation. Before I get started, I want you to remember two things. First, dishonest people can only operate if trust exists. As humans, we naturally default to believing the person is truthful. Unless there is overwhelming evidence of dishonesty, most people will give someone the benefit of the doubt and initially trust the person standing in front of them.

A classic example of this theory comes right before the start of World War II. In 1938, the Prime Minister of England, Neville Chamberlain, met with Adolf Hitler in Germany. Upon returning to England, Chamberlain was quoted as saying he had achieved "Peace for our time." The Munich agreement would guarantee this peace. The agreement stated that Germany could occupy the Sudetenland, the German-speaking part of Czechoslovakia, and that no more territorial demands in Europe would be made. After meeting with Hitler, Chamberlain was convinced that he could trust the man. Chamberlain defaulted naturally to Hitler as a truthful man. On the other hand, Winston Churchill, who had never met the man, knew that Hitler could not be trusted from the beginning. Churchill states,

> *We cannot tell whether Hitler will be the man who will once again let loose upon the world another war . . . or whether he will go down in history as the man who restored honor and peace of mind to the great Germanic nation.*[10]

---
10 Patrick J. Buchanan, Churchill, Hitler, and "The Unnecessary War": How Britain Lost Its Empire and the West Lost the World (Forum Books, 2009), 173-174.

How could these two extremely smart individuals have such differences of opinion? I believe Churchill sums it up,

> Those who have met Herr Hitler face to face... have found a highly competent, cool, well-informed functionary with an agreeable manner, a disarming smile, and few have been unaffected by a subtle personal magnetism.[11]

If you met Adolf Hitler, it seems his ability for you to believe he is telling the truth is highly evolved by his charisma and charm. However, Churchill did not believe Hitler was an honorable man and was not deceived by his words. He could gather from Hitler's own writings and policies what his intentions were.

> **WHEN A LIE BECOMES MULTI-LAYERED AND ELABORATE, THAT THICKENED BLACK STROKE ON YOUR LIFE'S CANVAS WILL EVENTUALLY BE SEEN FOR WHAT IT IS.**

In bringing this story back to my point, our ability to believe that a person's normal behavior is to be truthful can lead to manipulation if we do not understand ourselves and our own gut feelings. If you are the manipulator, you rely on this trust to keep your lies going. Holiday time really puts this to the test. (Of note, I understand not allowing others to control your life. There are times you will need to rebel and fight for what you believe

---
11 Buchanan, Churchill, Hitler, and "The Unnecessary War". 173.

is the right decision. However, sometimes you should listen to those around you who may not be under the veil of truth default. In certain situations, listen to those whom you respect and know have your best interest in mind. They may just be your Churchill trying to help you avoid a long, drawn-out war and instead pursue the divine purpose for your life.)

The second point I want to make before I begin my story is that lie begets lie. You never know what you are capable of devising until you have to continue weaving a pattern of deceit. We each create a canvas of our lives. We paint ourselves for the world and allow others to look at our work and either agree or disagree with who we are. Each action we take is like a brush stroke. Whether the brushstroke is a reality or a lie, it all goes onto our canvas for anyone to see. The closer we get to someone, the closer they look at our brush strokes. Taking the example further, let's assume a lie is a black stroke. From a distance, a few strokes of black would hardly be recognizable. A significant area of black may be recognizable from afar but still may prove difficult. However, the closer someone gets to you, the easier it will be to see. When a lie becomes multi-layered and elaborate, that thickened black stroke on your life's canvas will eventually be seen for what it is. Let's begin. . . .

It was Christmas Eve 2010. I had been divorced for a few years and it was not my first Christmas without the kids. My kids were getting older, and the excitement of elf on the shelf and Santa Claus was fading with each passing year. As the magic was fading from my children's hearts, so had the light inside of me for the holiday season faded. I had been seeing two women at the same time for a few months now. Neither woman knew anything about the other, and I was going to keep it that way. In fact, I was going to keep it that way regardless of the cost. In my eyes, each woman, very different in character, possessed something I thought I needed. One was extremely accepting and caring, and I enjoyed her company. She was the stability in my life and brought me peace. The other was strong-willed, sexual, and opinionated. She was the catalyst that showed me just what I was capable of and because of the extremes we displayed together, the relationship was both exciting and filled with turmoil (more about this in a later chapter).

Understand, at this time in my life, I thought I was capable of anything. I was living a life of deception. I was feeding my ego by priding myself on having two beautiful women who thought the world of me. I exploited that trust and love to fulfill my own selfishness with no regard for either of their feelings. I did feel remorse toward my actions, but that was not going to stop this pattern and life I had created. I had the illusion of control over my life. I was arrogant, full of pride, and looked like I had it all. However, on the inside, I was eaten up with anxiety and chest pain daily.

The daily advent calendar leading up to Christmas Day is supposed to bring excitement, but I began to view it as the countdown to D-Day. Prior to Christmas Eve, I had made many decisions on what I was going to do for the holiday. Each woman wanted me to spend it with her. I could not say no to both, thus, the elaborate string of lies began. First, how do I spend time with both without the other knowing? Second, what kind of presents do I need? Third, is there any way out of this scenario? In the past, I would just go see my parents and I had the best excuse not to be somewhere, but that was not going to work this year.

The plan began to take shape over the next few weeks leading up to Christmas. I can remember going to a jewelry store and buying two very similar pieces. The awkward silence that I felt when I purchased both should have knocked me back to reality then. Next came the kids, buying presents for each, who were all around the same age, might I add. It was very important to make sure I did not confuse each present when I wrapped them. Confession: I actually did wrap a girl present in boy wrapping paper in my lack of concentration on the details and bought out of obligation instead of wanting to give. The little girl was not happy about that, and that mishap became a joke for her birthday a few months later.

So as the day got closer and closer, my plan took place. That year, Christmas looked like a scene from the movie *Four Christmases*.[12] I was going to make this work. I told both that I would be there with them. As I write this story, I think about all I have done over the years, and there were some real scumbag things. I am writing this now because I know some of you are currently doing something very similar to what I was about to do. Your situation may be different. It may be a wife to a girlfriend. It may be New Year's, but none of those details matter. Realize that it sucks and will only get worse as the years go on.

It was finally Christmas Eve. I ended up deciding to spend the night with my "emotional" woman, as I figured there would be less messaging from my "peaceful" woman. So, the holiday officially began with a screenshot of a thermometer I had put in

---

12 Seth Gordon, *Four Christmases* (November 26, 2008; Burbank, CA: New Line Cinema).

warm water. I was feeling "horrible" and "I did not want to get her family sick." I actually said that if I felt better tomorrow, I would love to see her.

As the night unfolded, I would constantly have to leave for a text. I would answer and deliver texts in the bathroom. I would text when I had to get a tool from the garage to help get her Santa Claus stuff ready for her kids. I would text when she would leave the room for any reason. What should have been a joyful time of celebration turned into a stressful nightmare. Bedtime had finally come, and it was time to attempt sleep despite my stomach burning a hole in itself. I can still remember that feeling and counting the minutes till daytime.

In the morning, I acted like all things were good. I knew that traditionally there are fewer texts in the morning, so I figured I could relax a little, but that was short-lived. I played the loving boyfriend and gave gifts. I sat around for an hour or so and said I wanted to get ready for Christmas dinner and I had to go home. I purposely did not bring any of my clothes or toiletries so I would be able to leave. It was my forgetfulness that made me forget to bring my stuff. Silly me!! I would be back soon, but soon led to hours.

When I left, I immediately called my "peaceful" woman and said I was feeling better. My thermometer read 98.6 degrees and I would love to see her and her family. I got ready and told "emotional" woman that my kids contacted me and wanted to see me. I would be back later that day but in time for dinner. Phase two had begun. We went to church, I gave presents, and we ate an early Christmas dinner. Everything was going great until I started receiving texts again asking where I was. Crap!! It was time to leave and so I lied that my kids wanted to see me despite me not having them that Christmas. Forty-five minutes later, I arrived for my second Christmas dinner within two hours' time. The day finished up and I finally went home. Rejoicing, I was through the holiday, but unfortunately, I had to start thinking about New Year's Eve and the string of lies I would have to concoct to make it through that one, too. The cycle continued.

By the time evening came on December 25th, I had been to church twice, opened two different sets of presents, eaten two Christmas dinners, never saw my own kids, and messaged each woman saying I had the best time and thank you for sharing it with me. I did have a great time knowing I got away with keeping my life compartmentalized and never truly building a long-lasting relationship. I continued living a life like that for some time but eventually, on top of a mountain, with my dog, and alone, my heart grew two sizes one day. It was this growth that gave me the strength to write this story.

Key Point:

To succeed, I utilized the classic deception technique of truth default. Even though the story is so farfetched, even though both those women were smart and intelligent, they had no overwhelming evidence not to trust me. I would later find out that it was their families who spotted the red flags. The story just seemed too crazy for them to believe. Their families were not shrouded in the veil of deceit. They started dropping seeds of mistrust and they were right to do so. Those relationships ended badly, and I still feel the pain of what I did. Forgiveness and true repentance have occurred, but the memory still remains.

I want to apologize for the deception of my past to these two women. I want them to know that these lessons and stories are going to help others grow. I want them to know that what was intended for bad, God has turned around for His purpose in helping others not fall into this same trap. I do hope forgiveness can be achieved, if not already done so.

TIME OF CELEBRATION

When it comes to a holiday, what is not to like? Well actually, a lot, if you are living a life of lies, manipulation, and selfishness. As I write, I am reminded of Jude 1:23, "*Save others by snatching them from the fire; to others show mercy, mixed with fear——hating even the clothing stained by corrupted flesh.*" I am going to reveal the magic tricks. Smoke, mirrors, and sleight of hand. No more looking over here while someone is taking from over there. I do this so that all will be educated. I do this so the truth can push back the darkness. I want to expose the tactics so that we may find freedom. If you are the manipulator, you are panicking right now. Good. You should be panicking. I intend to show you mercy, but I hope some fear is building up. I do not want you to go so far down the wrong path that it takes years to find your way back. On the other hand, if you think you are being manipulated, let me help you see the patterns and look at the bigger picture. Let me tell you what the manipulator does not want you to know. Let me help you out of the fire that you have found yourself surrounded by. What you do with this information is entirely up to you.

Holidays will be the best time to reveal the truth. If you, the manipulated, have a feeling in the pit of your stomach, this would be the time to check your suspicions. However, I do caution you; this has the possibility of ruining the holiday if any information does in fact surface. If the manipulator feels trapped or out of control, it will also most likely incite rage or anger. Without further delay:

Holidays Force You to Deviate from Your Normal Routine
Manipulator: The schedule is what allows you to remember the lies you tell. Disrupting your normal routine draws attention to yourself, and this can get you caught.
Manipulated: Something will be very off. Weird visits to the gas station for batteries or constant quick disappearances for something. For someone who is usually very calculated, they will appear unprepared or forgetful.

Holidays Force Increased Communication
Manipulator: Your mind will always race. You can never be in the present. There is minimal relaxation, and your conversations will be shallow. Most of the time the holiday will end in turmoil, and you will hear something similar to, "Aren't you listening to me?"
Manipulated: When communication takes place, there will be very few details. You may find yourself saying the same thing twice or perhaps three times. Try to get them to speak in detail. The more the better. Since, to you, the truth is what you hear, you will have no problems remembering, but they will have a difficult time remembering. Make a point to have multiple things stand out. Journaling and writing down events on napkins have proven helpful for me to keep track of what was said, in detail. A manipulator is great at getting you to doubt yourself on certain events.

If there are multiple events and you defer on how you see them and what you are told, I promise you are not crazy.

Holidays Force You to Reconnect Unwillingly

Manipulator: This is the last thing you want. You have created a life that compartmentalizes who you are. When you are forced to reconnect, this begins to blur the compartments.

Manipulated: You will notice that no matter what you do, they will find some way to ruin the holiday. It will be something so trivial that it makes no sense. When everything is going great, they must find a way to prevent this. The manipulator will make sure it all goes "well enough". "Well enough" keeps things in the gray zone. When there is just enough tension in the room, the manipulator doesn't have to reconnect.

Holidays Have the Potential to Destroy Your Second Life: Enter Social Media

Manipulator: Here's the game you play. You come off social media for a bit to hide your online activity. In this way, not only do you evade the risk of being tagged (thereby blowing your cover), but you are now free to maintain those forbidden relationships. People love to post about their life, especially during the holidays. Because you know this is very dangerous ground, you devise a plan to avoid it.

Manipulated: Post away. You are happy to be spending time with those you love. If a partner comes off social media, ask yourself why. Is it around their birthday so that messages can't be shared on their board? Are you going on a special vacation, and all of a sudden, they need a break from social media? Remember, there are times when people truly need a break from social media. This does not mean there is something wrong but look for patterns. If your gut is telling you something is not quite right, perhaps you should listen.

IN THE END . . .

Holidays are meant to be a time of celebration. I understand that they are stressful. However, they can be very rewarding if we truly take a break from the day-to-day routine of our lives and enjoy the essence and atmosphere each holiday brings. In my former life, I never could relax enough to enjoy the holidays. I was always concerned that my ruses would be uncovered. The intricate string of lies stole most of the joy I could have had if I had made better choices and lived an honest and transparent life.

When I look back on some of the holidays I experienced, I can do nothing but lower my head and sigh. So much time was wasted, but some hard lessons have been learned. Do not repeat my mistakes. Start walking away from things that do not bring you peace. If you cannot be transparent, then what you are doing will absolutely change the way you view holidays. I know this sounds cliché (even typing it makes me sound like a fortune cookie). As someone who has walked this path and found true freedom, holidays have never been better. I have learned to celebrate each holiday in a way I have never known. I can say with certainty that God does repay the years that the locust has eaten.

HARD TRUTH #5
A BEAUTIFUL WOMAN CAN PULL YOUR PUPPET STRINGS.

"Like a gold ring in a pig's snout is a beautiful woman who shows no discretion."
Proverbs 11:22

Stories portraying seduction and sexuality have been luring men and women to their death for thousands of years. Every culture throughout history has tried to explain sexuality and what it can do. In Greek mythology, the song of the sirens has been famously known since Homer orated the Odyssey.[13] A siren was a woman with an irresistible allure and could enchant a man with her song. Once enchanted, the men would lose their lives at the sirens' bird-claw feet. It was here that they died blissfully, ecstatically, and in a state of sexual pleasure. Likewise, Shakespeare's character, Lady Macbeth, famously manipulates her husband into committing murder so she can enhance her quest

---
13 Homer, "The Odyssey".

for power.[14] All throughout literature, women have been manipulating men; however, women are not alone in their seduction.

Literature does not discriminate. Men have the power to seduce a woman, as one Irish folklore describes. The Irish Gancanagh "Love Talker" is a male fairy who secretes a toxin from his skin that makes the women he seduces addicted to him. Once addicted, he withdraws his toxin and watches, as he can now influence the women addicted to him. An even greater tragedy is that they die by their own hands from the withdrawal of this toxin or will fight to the death with other women for his love. Likewise, in Scottish mythology, the Elfin Knight seduces young women from their beds, and they end up at the bottom of an icy river. They are attracted to his perceived bravery, charm, and nobility. However, this deception ends up leading to their death.

What do these stories tell us? Why do they all sound like a potential Netflix series but instead of fairies and sirens, The antagonist would now be classified as a narcissist, Jezebel, or sociopath? The answer is that beauty has a way of blinding us from the truth if used in conjunction with manipulation. So, the questions are: Are beautiful men and women bad? Should seduction and passion be avoided? My answer to these questions is, God, I hope not!!! That would be a terrible conclusion. However, can seduction, beauty, or sexuality create disorder in our lives? Do these desires sometimes override what we know to be truth? Do these cravings change something inside of us that intoxicates us to the point that long-term consequences for our actions become irrelevant? The answer to all of these? You bet your ass they do.

---

14 William Shakespeare, Macbeth, 1.7.

THE SCIENCE OF ATTRACTION

A well-dressed middle-aged man is sitting in Starbucks drinking his nitro cold brew. He looks up and, at that moment, he sees a woman with blonde hair, red lipstick, and curvy in all the places he desires. She looks like an older version of his high school girlfriend who broke up with him when they left for college. He has no idea why he is attracted or drawn to her; he just knows he wants her. At this point, what is he willing to do? Would he risk embarrassment or the pain of rejection if she does not feel or think the same way?

For the sake of the story, let us assume she does feel the same way. She was instantly attracted to him since she previously dated a man whom she loved many years ago and who always kissed her after drinking his nitro cold brew. So not necessarily understanding why, she comes over and talks to him. The conversation leads to smiles and laughs. The hormones begin surging and they begin to mimic each other's movements. The similarities are uncanny, and this is the first excitement that either has felt in months. He thinks, "My wife is just so plain. She doesn't make me laugh anymore. She uses me as a meal ticket." Likewise, she thinks to herself, "This man is truly listening to me. We are on a wavelength with a connection that I do not have with my husband." They exchange numbers, and eighteen months later, the private investigator discovers the affair.

What happened in this story? On the surface, you see two bored people with a perceived misunderstanding of their spouses. They meet each other serendipitously as if God destined this meeting. On a deeper level, you might ask, why these two? What changed inside of them that overrode their ability to care about the long-term consequences of their actions? This is just one of many reasons that people study the science of attraction. What makes people do stupid things for beauty?

Our explanation of attraction begins in the limbic system. The limbic system is classically described as our primitive brain. As our primitive brain operates, it is responsible for physical hunger, protection, reproduction, and a host of other purposes. When we see someone attractive, our limbic system floods our brains with dopamine and serotonin. The happy chemicals are released, and our bodies start producing a chemical called oxytocin. This oxytocin (the bonding chemical) starts changing the makeup of our brains and, collectively, these hormones go to work. They work so well that they can override the higher levels of thinking. Translation: I want it now and I don't care how. What happens in the long term is irrelevant.

Awesome, but why did my limbic system start producing these chemicals in such large quantities? Why do I view this person as my dream woman or man? Why am I willing to risk it all to be with this person at all costs? The answer to this question is a bit complicated, but to simplify it, it is because of our collection of experiences, culture, and biology. Cutting through all the science jargon, self-help books, cosmopolitan surveys, and TikTok advice, attraction can be summed up in three properties all with varying degrees of importance based on the context:

1) Similarities
2) Proper ratios
3) Cultural stigma from family and friends

Similarities

These similarities can be reminders of loved ones, past relationships, or friends. Equally important is that similarities are strong indicators of attractiveness. We tend to be attracted to those who share similar affinity across the five personality traits. These traits are extroversion, conscientiousness, agreeableness, neuroticism, and openness. Likewise, studies show that approximately three-fourths of marriages have partners who share the same political affiliation and religious beliefs. We like what we like and search for what is most familiar to us.

Proper Ratios

Regardless of how much you try to deny it, what our eyes see plays a big role in our attraction decision. I am sure that most of you have heard of the Golden Ratio. This ratio describes symmetry across all of nature and plays a role in distinguishing what is a beautiful face and what is not. Although there is some debate on whether the Golden Ratio is important in what is found to be beautiful, other ratios have proven to be supported by science. Let's just say that our biology, regardless of how great our personality is, can sometimes override what we find attractive. One example is a 70 percent waist-to-hip ratio of a woman predicts increased attractiveness to a man. Likewise, another study demonstrated that a certain curvature of the spine was found attractive to certain men because it allows for more successful birthing of children. The reality is that individual attraction changes based upon certain physical attributes, and to deny that is folly. I have heard the arguments that what I look like on the inside should matter more than how I look. It sure does, but what you look like on the outside matters on a level that very few people truly understand. In the words of Ron Burgundy, "It's science."[15]

Cultural Stigma from Society, Family, and Friends

The media has unspeakable power over our lives. We are consistently and unknowingly being told what to think, feel, and believe. Our version of truth is being molded and formed sometimes without our cognitive awareness. By applying this logic, the pursuit of what is considered beautiful is culturally driven and subjective. This means that society has a significant influence on what we consider beautiful and is subject to change over time.

In western societies, the 1920s began to change the definition of beauty. It was then that "plump" began falling out of societal norms when beauty standards in magazines and movies began highlighting thinness as beautiful to both men and women. Flat stomachs, chiseled jawlines, and hourglass figures became societal norms and continue to be to this very day. However, history is not all lost. The plump trend still exists in certain areas of the world. In Mauritania, a western African country, women are force-fed to maintain fat as this is considered beautiful amongst the men of this country. A woman who is considered plump implies fertility and a sign of wealth. This phenomenon of cultural norms dictating "beauty" plays a key factor in ourself-perception of beauty.

Likewise, those closest to us have a strong presence in our lives by influencing our behaviors. Research has shown that a person is attracted to those with qualities that family/friends deem normal based on social constructs. These constructs usually dictate that an individual has found a beautiful person when he or she has

---

[15] Adam McKay, Anchorman: The Legend of Ron Burgundy (July 9, 2004; Los Angeles, CA: Apatow Productions).

found a considered equal to the beholder. Social status, age, race, height, and body type are all influential in the creation of the construct. This reasoning offers some insight into why trends change over the years. In 1980, 7 percent of marriages were considered interracial marriages. As of 2015, 17 percent of marriages are interracial.[16] The resulting changes could be perceived as altered social constructs as acceptance amongst family and friends continues to evolve. Although beauty is fleeting, family and friends will, to some degree, dictate our personal choice in what we consider beautiful, and that has the ability to change with time.

> YOU MUST UNDERSTAND, THOUGH, THAT WITHOUT SOMETHING ANCHORING YOU TO THE SHORE, THE WATER WILL JUST GET DEEPER AND DEEPER AS YOU KEEP TRYING TO FIND PERFECTION THAT WILL NEVER EXIST.

The English writer D. H. Lawrence wrote, "Beauty is an experience, nothing else. It is not a fixed pattern or an arrangement of features. It is something felt, a glow, or a communicated sense of fineness."[17] As your life changes, as you experience both good and bad things, your perceptions of the world will change. With this

---

16 Gretchen Livingston and Anna Brown, "Trends and Patterns in Intermarriage," Pew Research Center, 18 May 2017, https://www.pewresearch.org/social-trends/2017/05/18/1-trends-and-patterns-in-intermarriage/.
17 D. H. Lawrence, "Beauty is an experience, nothing else. It is not a fixed pattern or an arrangement of features. It is something felt, a glow, or a communicated sense of fineness," AZ Quotes, https://www.azquotes.com/quote/520328.

changed perception, your beliefs may also change. I have thought about my life and the stories I have been told by women and men about why they have cheated on or divorced their spouses. By far, the number one reason I have found when you pare down the fluff of not trying to sound shallow and selfish is, "I just don't find them attractive anymore." This simple statement brings clarity to me.

In these divorced couples, it was their unshared experiences that led to the first cracks in the ice. It was the bombarding influence, to the point of exhaustion, of what society considers beautiful that created the next cracks in the ice. However, the collapse into the cold, icy lake of seduction/sin occurred when they pursued their individualized absolute standard of beauty for that moment of their life. The one thing all who have taken this plunge have forgotten is that the pursuit has no end because your standard of beauty will never stay the same. Beauty is subjective, and a physical attribute or a personality trait that you find attractive may only be for a season in your life. You must understand, though, that without something anchoring you to the shore, the water will just get deeper and deeper as you keep trying to find perfection that will never exist. As you are hopping from one foot to the next, you will slowly or suddenly die a spiritual, emotional, or physical death trying to succeed. The marionette of your endless pursuit is just laughing watching you destroy those all around you for a little taste of your coworker. Oh, how easily we can be deceived. Enter manipulation. . . .

THE POWER OF BEAUTY TO MANIPULATE

This book will not use buzzwords to identify the culprit of manipulation or jealousy. I will charge you to search out your own heart to decide the reasoning and source. My goal is to bring to light the pain it causes and how easy it can be to fall victim to both conducting and being influenced by it.

"It is amazing how complete is the delusion that beauty is goodness." In 1890, Leo Tolstoy penned this quote in the controversial book, Kreutzer Sonata. The book gives a first-person account of the jealous rage of a man who suspects his wife is having an affair. The jealousy and manipulation consume him and drive him to murder his wife. The book ends with the husband realizing what he had done days later when he sees his wife's tomb and asks for forgiveness from the narrator of the book.[18] Although tragic, this book leads you into the mind of someone who can no longer control his actions when placed in a situation that confirmed the suspicions he had conjured in his mind. The book shines light on just how far things can go when jealousy or manipulation is involved.

Manipulation is a behavior that exploits, controls, or influences others to one's advantage. Manipulation can take place for a variety of reasons. For some, manipulation can be used to make them feel better about themselves. Others use it to gain power and influence to advance themselves. Still, others use it in a more sinister way to distract you from your purpose in life. Regardless of the reason, I believe that some know exactly what they are doing, and others who are just simply blinded to the influence they are exerting over another.

At some point in our lives, we have all manipulated someone for our own agenda. Our naturally selfish nature keeps us in a steady state of internal turmoil of doing what we know is right and pursuing our own ambitions regardless of the cost. Ambitions in

---
18 Leo Tolstoy, The Kreutzer Sonata (Berlin: Bibliographic Office, 1889).

themselves are not a bad thing. The idea of inventing, marrying a partner, creating value for society, or pursuing excellence in your craft are all admirable goals and should be encouraged. However, just as Jesus was tempted in the wilderness by three lusts of life, you will find that manipulation is successful when it seeks to distort one, two, or all three of these lusts to the victim.

Manipulation for the Flesh

Flesh... hearing the word just immediately triggers a response in me. I hear the word and I think of what I am not supposed to do. In Christian circles, flesh usually implies a negative connotation, but flesh is a good thing. When controlled and honoring to God, fleshly desires should be celebrated. Manipulation of the flesh is something entirely different. As discussed, manipulation exploits, controls, or influences for one's own advantage. Examples of the flesh include using your physical strength, sexual body, smooth speech, or seductive touch. The act of giving someone pleasure and controlling someone physically to get what you desire or advance your agenda is manipulation of the flesh.

Every one of us is guilty of this. How many times did you wear that shirt that was one button too low on a date because it was the last thing in your closet that was clean? Didn't think so. How many times have you complimented your boss on the way their hair looked knowing that, honestly, you couldn't care less what it looked like? Exactly. Although subtle, these are examples of manipulation. I can hear the trolls coming out from under the bridge now. "I wear that because it makes me feel good about myself." I am sure it does when you get the occasional glance by someone desiring to either touch or see what is underneath. Just be aware that some of your choices are not as harmless as you may think and may be chosen for manipulation. Sometimes doing the nice thing, if done unwillingly, can be manipulation.

Manipulation for the Eyes

It has been said the eyes are the gateway to the soul. References directed toward what we fix our eyes upon or look upon are scattered throughout the Bible. The eyes are symbolic in determining the path we are going to take. By manipulating the eyes, you can alter the path by littering it with false perceptions. These are the social media posts of the person who constantly takes pictures of their "stuff". New cars, new boats, new house. They manipulate people by altering their perception of status or importance to the world. The eyes have an insatiable desire to want what someone else has. In manipulating one's eyes, it is very possible that the manipulated may chase the things the manipulator has and will forsake their true purpose in pursuit of them.

Manipulation for Pride

Pride is patting yourself on the back for your achievements. You achieved success, gained power, or landed the girl on your own. Nobody helped you and you deserve all the things you have because you worked for it. You deserve the credit for the deal made. You deserve the position of authority. You deserve to let others know you are great.

Manipulating for pride is making yourself seem grander than you actually are. These are the people who somehow know everyone. You mention a name and they are friends with that person. These are the people who were in Special Forces in the military. I am honestly convinced that there is no one who has not been in special forces. These are the people who constantly have to tell you about all the things they have done on LinkedIn. I am going to share a secret: the one who is actually important will not tell you, show you, or post about it.

At this point, you may be asking yourself, what does beauty have to do with all of this? Well, let me show you. Picture the most beautiful person you can think of whom you actually know. (No celebrity crushes here. Let's keep this in the realm of what is possible.)

What would you do if they winked at you or touched you on the hand while smiling? Key your hormones. I do not care who you are, in that moment, you most likely are helpless and ready to be manipulated.

How would you feel if that person went on a trip to some tropical paradise and posted it? The thought of wanting to be there with that person may just pop up and jealousy or anger of desiring something you do not have may begin to dictate your life.

What would you think if they talked to you and told you about the people they have met while traveling the world? You will probably think you need to up your game so you can impress them because your life is too boring to get a partner like them.

I hope you can see how this works. Beauty has a way of lowering our defenses of expressing our authentic selves. In the context of this book, our defenses can be a multitude of mechanisms that we have instituted to live life a certain way. Examples could be: No physical touch, no after hours messaging, or never discussing relationships with the opposite sex. As all things begin with us, attractive people, if so inclined, can push those very boundaries and affect us, and the majority of the time, without consciously realizing it. Remember, the limbic brain can override the frontal brain—usually not at the most opportune time. Likewise, beauty can influence your impression of a person when you may have otherwise been warned to watch yourself. As our defenses are lowered, we begin to relax and trust people more readily based on appearance and not merit. This is the danger, and this is what research has called the "halo effect".

The halo effect is our brain's natural inclination to link one trait to drastically influence our perception of all other traits. If you think someone is beautiful, you are also likely to assume they're smart, ambitious, interesting, trustworthy, and exciting. Study after study has proven this effect as people are asked to rate character traits based on looks that overwhelmingly favor beautiful people. Examples in other fields include business, which has shown beautiful people earn more money, achieve more promotions, and are generally more employable. Being aware of the halo effect may be key to overcoming your own impulses to do what you know to be wrong. I advise caution moving forward so that human nature may not override your life, leaving you unable to make healthy decisions.

To sum it up, beauty has the power to influence, move us in certain directions, or open us up to things we never thought possible. The ability to not let beauty affect us goes against our natural instincts and can test our character to the core. When beauty begins to manipulate a desire within us, the effects become exponential as the ripples of our choices filter throughout our lives. This is exactly what happened to me as I went from a master of my own choices to a puppet of a beautiful woman.

THE WOMAN ON THE WATER

The first time I saw her, there was something different about her. When I say fulfillment, I truly meant it. She seemed to be sent as an answer to my life. At the time, I was overworked and underpaid. The fall was bringing cooler nights, and the days were getting shorter. The early setting of the sun was signifying a slowing down from the long summer days and relief to my mind as I thought, "I was missing the best years of my life." I was stressed about most everything and had zero time to enjoy any part of a miserable existence that I called my life. I was frustrated trying to keep afloat financially while supporting three kids that I barely saw. This mixture of envy for those around me and the sadness I felt of a life wasted became a perfect combination for what was to become.

She entered my life like a hurricane. She brought new experiences and flooded my mind with thoughts of a brighter future. She was able to support herself and paid for me during certain outings, and the gifts I received were the exact opposite of what I was used to. For years, I thought of myself as a meal ticket, trying to support a life that I did not get to enjoy. Nobody understood what I was struggling with, until refreshingly, she blew in, and I welcomed it (at first). The beginning brought a joy I had not felt in many years—things seemed to look a little brighter, smell a little better, and taste a little sweeter. However, just like with every storm, sometimes we forget the havoc that it causes despite the beauty of the moment. My house, or life, was built on shifting sand. I had drifted to a place that barely resembled a godly life, but I was in complete control. I was going to make it on my own with no counsel and no "awesome" or "praise the Lord" as every fifth word Christians used to tell me how to live. I had this, and my pride came before my fall. Little did I know, I and all I cared for were about to be washed out to sea in the whirlwind that would follow.

> I HAD BECOME THE PROPERTY OF A BEAUTIFUL WOMAN AND WAS UNAWARE OF WHAT SHE WAS GOING TO ASK OF ME.

The halo effect had taken over. I would brush off little things as annoying but cute in the beginning. With each passing day, the boundaries of my life would get smaller and smaller until they essentially became non-existent. I was willing to do anything for this woman and the cost of allowing this mindset to set in went from pocket change to diamonds in a hurry. I was tested intermittently to see just how far I would go. Once I was hooked like a junky looking to score my next hit, that's when the price of my decisions began to take shape. Every friend, family member, colleague, and counselor could see the turmoil developing. I was blinded by beauty and the thought of not having it sent me into a nosedive. Oh, there were chances to pull out of it, but I was entranced. The master puppeteer was pulling my strings, and I was going to dance awkwardly for the world to see. I had become the property of a beautiful woman and was unaware of what she was going to ask of me.

Children have a way of seeing things for what they are. They do not reason themselves to accept what is told to them. They do not get captivated by beauty as their brains are not affected by certain hormones. Feed them, love them, listen to them, and lead them is about it. Make them feel safe and wanted and you most likely cannot fail.

Life continued and the relationship developed. It was time to leave fantasyland, and the honeymoon phase ended. What better way to start than to introduce my children and begin to live life together? I began to incorporate my children into a life with this woman. I noticed subtle changes in her attitude, and it felt like a competition for my time had begun. I would begin to feel uneasy about the situation and when I got close to saying something, I would have a gift waiting for me and somehow would believe every passive-aggressive word spoken to me that my kids were the problem. Slowly, my children would begin to express that they would like to do something just with me, without her. Each time we were together, they seemed to become more fearful of having to spend time with her. At first, I thought she was great; maybe they just need to adjust since this is not mom. I kept reasoning with myself that everything was okay. I would find myself spending more and more time with her and less time with my kids. I would ask my kids to spend time with me, but they would politely tell me that they just want to stay with their mom. I would get frustrated with them and could not understand why they did not want to see me. The truth slowly started to be exposed and eventually began to open my eyes. The problem was that I was so hooked, I would tell myself I would get away, but I never did.

The truth began to reveal itself as she would withdraw affection from me if I spent time with my kids and did not choose her. I would find myself stressed out and having to plan everything down to the minute so I could optimize time. It was met with resistance, and I was constantly being told my actions were abandoning her and her family. I would cut holidays short; I would sleep three to four hours a night as I drove all over the state from her house to my house, from work to the kid's house. I became quick to anger, gaps began to cloud my memory, and rebellion in the form of dishonesty became my escape from the life I was still convinced was exactly what I wanted, and I had no idea why. All I knew was that the thought of her and her beauty with someone else would consume me and she made sure to play with my mind when I was not with her. Story after story of turmoil plagued this time in my life. Stories of me leaving a family trip to fly on a plane for twelve hours to see her and flying back the next day to be with my kids, all because she was not invited on the trip and was "going on a date." (Oh, and despite that gesture, she did still go out with that man.) Might I add, many months later, I was confronted by this man in a high school locker room during a wrestling match. Two forty-somethings about to fight in a locker room makes for an interesting story, but the escalation calmed down when we quickly realized we were both being lied to. The examples are endless as I played this game.

What I later came to believe was that the problem rested with me. I was constantly told that what I did was not enough. I was bleeding from a death of a thousand cuts and my health, relationships with those I loved, and work began to suffer. Still, there was no way I was going to leave all this. The days turned into months.

Months turned into years and the body count of those I hurt along the way mounted. All my relationships became estranged, and my parents threatened to take my children permanently away from me in court if I continued down this path. I would leave her and go back. And leave her and go back. Over and over this cycle continued and I would destroy those around me. It wasn't until one day, on the lake I moved to for her, away from my kids, that I finally began to cut the strings that had made me dance to an endless song of agony.

Water is a dangerous wonder. It brings life but can take it away. It can clean but also dirty. It can bring joy and it can bring fear. The property of water a person experiences depends upon their current state. I was on the water looking for answers. I knew that life had become so chaotic that I looked forward to death. In fact, I welcomed it. I never would have taken my own life, but I wouldn't care if God called me home. Each and every day. To my chagrin, I was still here. For many years, I had been in a mindset of war. I was tired, broken, and felt no peace. I had drifted so far that I did not recognize the man in the mirror. Something happens to a person when this point is reached. Small whispers began to turn into screams and on the water that day, it finally began to make sense. The time had come for me to make bold changes in life. I would hear, "What you heard in your mind on the water lied to you and you don't get off that easy. You just cannot walk away." So, I still view what happened next as a pivotal time in shaking me back to reality.

I remember coming off the lake and proceeding to cook a seafood boil. As my one-hundred-gallon Old Bay seasoned boiling water pot was cooking those beautiful crab legs, the unthinkable happened. I remember the moment I saw it; my son was throwing a ball with his friend. The throw was wild and headed directly into those scrumptious crab legs. My son hit the pot and as to keep him from being soaked with the boiling water, I caught the pot barehanded and pulled it over onto me. Time stood still for a second and then I felt it. It splashed all over me, causing second-degree burns all over my face, arms, and chest. I was in agony for days, but that was trivial compared to what I had felt for years. I was going to make a solid change in my life, and I had come to realize that burn was the final pain I needed to push me to my breaking point for transformation.

So once the burns healed, I left everything and retreated to my cave. I called my assistant, parents, and kids to tell them I was going away for some time, and I did not know when I would be back. "Please do not worry about me, as this is something I must do." I got in my car and left my life. I spent forty days in my wilderness, resting, gaining perspective, and drawing strength. This journey will look different for everyone. This is just what worked for me.

When the time finally came to re-enter the world, I was ready. I quit the job that I got for her. I sold the house that I got for her. I began breaking myself from a life that I had interwoven for years. The months spent cleaning up my life were the hardest "cutting" I had done thus far. She was not going down without a fight. She bombarded me to try and make me jealous. When that didn't work, it was seduction. When that didn't work, it was intimidation. Likewise, the same tactics became almost laughable as they got recycled and re-purposed in a different package. I had to confront and deal with what put me there in the first place. It was dealing with myself that broke the spell. I was powerless to confront her but by dealing with my own issues, I was able to block all attempts to control and latch on. That is the key to freedom. I promise you, if you keep playing their game, you will never win. Life becomes worse and worse, despite what you think. There is no running from it because you can't outrun yourself. That lesson was hard and took years to learn. The key to victory lived within me and when I stepped into that position of authority again, the halo effect shattered. I was able to see it all for what it was. I could see what my children saw. I could see what my family saw. I could see what God saw. You think a beautiful woman by your side is amazing? Try having true freedom. That aphrodisiac, given from the One greater than you, is intoxicating and fulfilling in a way that no "10" could ever compare to.

The time has come to cut the strings holding you back. Pay attention to what is not being said around you. Release who you are at that moment and concentrate on who you want to be. Beauty changes as your experiences grow. Your human nature has a powerful effect that no one is immune to. It is time we stopped living in shame and quit worrying about what others may think. Since time began, this battle has been raging and will be here long after you are gone. I can assure you that seduction in one form or another will find you. Seduction can be sexual, financial, a promise of power, or acceptance into a group that you have longed to be a part of. Your story may be different, but I can assure you the motive is the same. You can put lipstick on a pig but guess what, it is still a pig. What you are seeking is not beauty; it is purpose. Focus on this and you may just avoid the beauty trap.

HARD TRUTH #6

YOU WILL NEVER KEEP UP WITH THE JONES'S.
They Can't Even Keep Up with Themselves.

> *"Do not wear yourself out to get rich; do not trust your own cleverness. Cast but a glance at riches, and they are gone, for they will surely sprout wings and fly off to the sky like an eagle."*
> Proverbs 23:4-5

Wealth is traditionally regarded as how much money you have accumulated. A diversified portfolio of stocks, real estate, tangible assets, and free cash all determine, to the average person, whether you are wealthy or not. Although money does play a part in wealth, studies have shown that "being wealthy" is something more internal. Most wealthy individuals (assets > one million dollars) define wealth differently. To these individuals, wealth is defined as emotional well-being that brings happiness and peace of mind. This means that their actual net worth means less than their emotional state of having it.

As we further examine wealth, studies have shown that the top three reasons for wealth accumulation in those who are wealthy may shock you. The ability to live comfortably, to have financial freedom, and to provide for their families and community are the keys to their success. I was shocked that the studies did not include flexing a Lambo as one of the reasons for attaining wealth. I did not read it was to make them feel better about themselves or gain status. I did not notice it was to land the hot girl and make others envious. This is an interesting concept of something that goes completely against what society would have you believe. Society focuses on the consumption of wealth to bring happiness, but this cannot be further from the truth. Let me further blow your mind with a few important statistics that will help me bring together my point:

Eighty percent of wealthy people are first-generation affluent; the average age is late 50s, and the majority drive a car that is between three to six years old.

Ninety-five percent of wealthy people are married with one spouse usually making greater than 80 percent of the income.

Ninety percent of wealthy families lose their wealth by the third generation.[19]

When we look at all these facts together, we see something interesting. First, wealth appears to be attainable to the average person if the reason for attaining the wealth is to obtain financial freedom or to provide for your family/community. Second, wealth is created more easily if you build it with one person who shares similar ideas on the purpose of wealth. Third, wealth tends

---

19 Thomas Stanley, The Millionaire Next Door: The Surprising Secrets of America's Wealthy (Lanham, MD: Taylor Trade Publishing, 2010).

to sprout wings and fly like an eagle with each passing generation. Lastly, if you work hard to play hard, use money to show off, or live with no true purpose but to feed your own desires, you can be assured that your chances of accumulating or maintaining true wealth will diminish.

MONEY VS TIME PARADOX

In the Bible, the most well-known verse on money, "The love of money is the root of all evil," (1 Timothy 6:10, author paraphrase) describes our fascination with money. As described above, money and wealth can open doors of opportunity, but what if we were to shift our focus away from money? Instead of working to obtain money, let's focus on working to accumulate TIME.

Time is finite. Every one of us has a certain amount of it. We cannot take it back nor gain more in the span of our lives. Time is marked by a beginning and an end. Based on your belief, time may mean something different. This book will not debate time's nature, what the flow of time is, nor what equates to fulfillment of time. Instead, I will talk about time as meaningfully moving forward. Meaningfully moving forward means that time will always flow from past to present and present to future. What you choose to do with the time allotted to you at any point depends entirely on you.

Time-centric individuals tend to have a different outlook on life. They tend to be happier, have healthier relationships, and have greater job satisfaction. Studies have shown that people who work for money become obsessed that they are doing worse in life as they compare what they have to their peers. The cycle of working for money and true fulfillment seems to elude them.

However, the idea of working for time and not money seems to be able to lift the burden of comparison and frees your focus on building wealth for happiness instead of accumulating it for selfish ambitions. Examples of this concept can be found all around you. Let me show you a simple example.

Picture it is a Saturday morning, and your son has a soccer game. You have missed the last two weeks because of work. You can never find the time to attend his games because money is your goal. You know the memories that could be created for both you and your son are priceless, but you really need to clean your house. Today is the day that you finally have a chance to do that. You have an overwhelming feeling that you have to go, so you do, but grudgingly. You feel the time lost will set you back in completing what you know you must do. Now, shift your focus to time creating happiness. You decide to hire a housecleaner with the money earned to create free time. This time gained creates those memories and increases your life satisfaction, leaving no regrets in the future.

> **JUST LIKE WITH ANY MUSCLE THAT HYPERTROPHIES (INCREASES IN SIZE), YOU HAVE TO START LIGHT BEFORE YOU CAN LIFT HEAVY.**

This simple story shows the concept of working for time. I realize that this concept may be foreign to most as you labor day in and day out to accumulate money. To change your mindset, I recommend starting slowly. Just like with any muscle that hypertrophies (increases in size), you have to start light before you can lift heavy. Begin by reminding yourself of your values and reflecting on why you are doing what you are doing. This does not mean evaluating your priorities. A value is an internal concept that judges what is important in your life. A priority is something that is regarded as more important than another. When you fall into the comparison trap, you tend to act upon your priorities, and your values begin to diminish. Likewise, begin to plan weeks, months, and years in advance to have more time to do what you find significant to your overall happiness by staying true to your values. When we can dissociate from the present thought of priority in the moment, freedom tends to find its way into our life.

WHAT WEALTH IS NOT AND THE NEVER-ENDING TREADMILL

Wealth is not the ability to purchase everything and anything you desire. Desires come and go throughout your life and buying the latest and greatest feeds desires that will most likely change in six months. Although the pleasure you feel in the moment may give you the boost of dopamine your brain craves, the cycle of wanting, getting, and wanting more will keep you locked in a battle that consumes your energy, time, and overall happiness in life.

Psychology calls this cycle the hedonic treadmill. The theory states that as you accumulate more of something, your expectations and desires rise in tandem with what you accumulate. A person will quickly return to a set level of happiness, but that set level will be higher than before. Conclusion: You can never achieve a greater level of happiness because your happiness will always remain in the same place. Yes, there will be increases and decreases in your perceived happiness but in the long term, happiness will remain the same.

Hedonism is defined as the pursuit of pleasure through self-indulgence. Pleasure in itself is not a bad thing. A good steak, a comfortable car, or a nice robe in a five-star resort can bring pleasure. God is not against pleasurable things. This is a common misconception that seems to penetrate the church. People talk about the pastor who buys a nice home like it is a bad thing. I have heard others state that those in Christian leadership have no business possessing such expensive cars in their lives. Why do we think that? Psalm 16:11 (ESV) states, "You make known to me the path of life; in your presence there is fullness of joy; at your right hand are pleasures forevermore." God Himself makes it known that He delights in giving you the desires of your heart as long as it aligns with His will in your life. Psalm 149:4 (ESV) tells us, "For the Lord takes pleasure in his people; he adorns the humble with salvation." This verse states how God experiences pleasure. With that stated, the desire for pleasure inside of you was placed there by Him for you to experience. Pleasure is not a bad thing, but we must distinguish between a godly pursuit of it versus a selfish pursuit. The problem occurs when you seek pleasure on your own accord to fulfill your own selfish desires. That is the heart of hedonism.

A treadmill is a device of torture for most people. You can walk, crawl, shuffle, jog, or run until the machine breaks but you will never go anywhere. When you finish your thirty minutes of pain, you are still in the same place. Sure, you may feel better about what you accomplished, but the fact remains—you are exactly where you started. As time goes on, you will have to increase your speed or time to get more of a workout. Likewise, the hedonic treadmill keeps you in the same place but to get the same effect as the day before, something has to increase. The cycle goes like this:

Desire—*I perceive I want something that I do not have.*
Strive—*I will do something to obtain that desire.*
Obtain—*I get that selfish desire and am instantly happy.*
Enjoy—*I will have fun for a period of time playing with that desire.*
Adapt—*I realize that my happiness in the desire is fading.*
Desire More—*I have to upgrade my current level of pleasure.*
Desire—*I perceive I want something that I do not have.*

I hope you can see the clear pattern. No amount of money can bring you happiness. The endless pursuit of money can't buy happiness. What you sacrifice to earn the extra dollar might not be for a reason that brings gratification to your life. If you are pursuing money and not true wealth, you may have to examine your reason and make changes. I know this personally and painfully.

THE ONE-HUNDRED-HOUR WORK WEEK

I was addicted to work. The hit came every two weeks as the paycheck would flex my bank account. I was making a ridiculous amount of money but what I did with the money, I still do not know. As I worked for money, the blur of the world passing around me seemed to consume every dollar I made. Mortgage payments, car payments, water bills, and endless entertainment seemed to continuously drain me financially every month with no end in sight. I kept telling myself that the next month would be different. I would work more and would finally end positive for once. That would be the way out, but that path never found its way to me.

At this time in my life, I was constantly living a lifestyle to impress. I had two houses, two cars, and a motorcycle, and would spend money on anything and everything. To say I was happy would be telling a lie, but I sure did make everyone believe I had this great life. I had saved nothing; I was spending money to impress women and thought I was living the dream. Restaurant owners knew my name, my girlfriends would have the latest tech devices and a wardrobe to match, but my kids had holes in their clothes. My priorities were skewed in a way I never thought possible. My hedonistic lifestyle had to be fed and I did not care how. I was seeking acceptance from those who couldn't care less how much I worked. Just like locusts, these people would use me, drain me of everything, and then move on. Did I care? Sure didn't. The envy of those around me, or so I thought, was what I sought.

> SOMETHING INSIDE MUST CHANGE FOR THIS FREEDOM TO BE OBTAINED AND THERE IS NO SHORTCUT.

Something happens to a person when they believe the key to financial independence is working more and more. The thought of changing my priorities never occurred to me for years to come. Oh sure, I heard the experts tell me that I should cut back on spending—don't buy that five-dollar coffee and bring your lunch to work. Although this advice may help, just like with every addiction, unless the mindset changes, this advice is useless. Financial independence cannot occur regardless of the number of trips you make to Starbucks. Something inside must change for this freedom to be obtained and there is no shortcut. However, I was convinced I could find it.

When I first started to evaluate my spending, I looked at how I was living. First, I decided that my travel expenses would be the first to decrease. I sold my motorcycle after a wreck that broke my hip. The story behind that can be summed up in one sentence: I was leaving from somewhere I never should have been. When I had recovered, I took the next step of trading an expensive car for one that was more practical. However, with the excess money I was saving, I just blew that on the lifestyle I had created.

Next, I decided I had to get rid of a dwelling. This second house was used as a staging area to live an alternative life. I would drink, party, and spend money on this place trying to turn it into my second home. There was no end to my pride as I would try to impress everyone I would bring there. It was stocked with the best of everything. Although I never received mail there, this place became my "bachelor pad." My hangout would further feed my hedonism. When I decided to get rid of this place, I thought this was a great step to conquering my money problem. Well, as you probably guessed, the money saved still did nothing to fix my financial situation, as I spent the money on trips out of town to feed the lifestyle. In fact, this probably ended up costing me more.

Next, I figured my problems came from the money I was spending on women. I was trying to impress with game tickets, luxury trips, clothing, jewelry, and anything else they wanted. This was going to be the solution to my problem. So, I decided that I was going to find someone I would not have to spend money on. I would find someone who could support herself. In fact, I was so convinced this was the way to financial freedom that I entered into toxic relationships. These toxic relationships fed me over and over again. I had become so addicted to these relationships, I found myself becoming the locust. I would take and take, giving little in return. However, just like everything else, my financial situation did not improve. I would forget to pay my own bills or spend money on useless things that brought no real value to my life. I became so entrenched into a lifestyle I had not earned nor was blessed with that to leave was stupid, despite the writing on the wall that indicated I should. I was on the treadmill and was running myself into the ground. The day of freedom never came despite my best efforts to curb my spending. My priorities were out of whack. It was not until I was on the verge of bankruptcy, working one-hundred-hour weeks, spending thousands of dollars on counselors and therapists, with nothing to show for my labors, that the light finally came on.

    I wish I could say the light blinded me. What started as a small flicker around me eventually became brighter and brighter. There was never an "ah-ha" moment but when I started to evaluate my values, that is when the patterns began to shift. So, the first thing I did was determine how to slow my spending by taking a closer look at the values I had pushed down. I had to spend time figuring out exactly what I believed in.

    How did I begin to change my values? Well, the first thing I did was determine what was important in my life. I began to talk to those around me and realized I had been absent from those I loved for a long time. I knew it would take time to rekindle those relationships. I was determined to rise above my current lifestyle but also terrified that I would fall back easily into the life I had lived for years. With much thought and prayer, I determined I had to take responsibility for something other than myself. My children only lived with me every other weekend, so I needed a way to ground my life. I needed something that relied on me every day regardless of what I was doing. At the sincere request of my daughter and after reading Proverbs 12:10, "The righteous care for the needs of their animals, but the kindest acts of the wicked are cruel," I got Sansa. I know this sounds ridiculous, but I had to start somewhere. Little did I know, she was exactly what I needed.

Sansa is 10 percent German Shepard and 90 percent velociraptor. She required constant attention, training, and a lot of food. This meant there was less time for spending and tomfoolery. I began spending my hours at night making sure she appeared happy. Those who have dogs know exactly what I am talking about. Although the appearance of her happiness is likely projected to my conscious by my own mind, something stirs in you when they look at you like an ASPCA commercial. Regardless of the looks I would get, I began noticing that my attention, wants, and needs began to focus less and less on me. It was subtle at first, with fewer nights out, fewer vacations away, and finding myself wanting to be home. The outside world of hedonism began to slowly become less important. It was in these moments—slowly, at first—that I found myself beginning to gain perspective on my life. I realized that it took something outside of me to force me to stop living a certain way and gain clarity on my values.

> **YOU ARE RESPONSIBLE FOR FINDING WHAT WILL SHAKE YOU FROM A SELFISH PURSUIT TO ONE THAT ALTERS YOUR ENTIRE LIFE TO GAIN FREEDOM.**

I am not saying everyone needs to get a dog. I understand allergies, constant vacuuming, and waking up to a butt in your face letting you know it's time to go out is not for everyone. The point I am making is that you must find something that will re-arrange your priorities. If you are like me, prayer time, Bible reading, or promise-making are all things that sound good in principle. However, if you are tired, you will be tempted to skip all of these. You'll tell yourself that you will do it later, but guess what, if you are in the place I was, you most likely won't. You are responsible for finding what will shake you from a selfish pursuit to one that alters your entire life to gain freedom.

I am thankful to say that wealth no longer invades me. I understand what brings me happiness, and it is not what society tells me. The emotional freedom I have, the ability to securely provide, and living a life that honors God have made the difference in providing me with true happiness. I understand that money is a part of living. There's no denying this statement. Still, one last statistic shows something very interesting. Research has shown that amongst those living in North America, approximately $75,000 a year brings emotional well-being and plays a pivotal role in keeping a person from unhappiness in regard to financial predictors.[20] Anything more may slightly increase for a person's happiness but not to the same effect as to $75,000. The sooner you truly realize that money will not make you happy, the sooner you will accumulate wealth. Remember, what you choose to spend it on, how you choose to work for it, or who you are using it for will determine your actual wealth level, and only you can make these choices. So, choose wisely, my friend, and don't get stuck on the treadmill chasing happiness from money.

---

20 Matthew A. Killingsworth, Daniel Kahneman, and Barbara Mellers, "Income and emotional well-being: A conflict resolved," Proc. Natl. Acad. Sci. 107, no. 38 (July 4, 2010), https://www.pnas.org/doi/10.1073/pnas.2208661120.

HARD TRUTH #7:
RIP OFF THE BAND-AID.
You Can't Escape Your Reality.

> *"And the God of all grace, who called you to his eternal glory in Christ, after you have suffered a little while, will himself restore you and make you strong, firm, and steadfast."*
> 1 Peter 5:10

Pain is a part of life. Pain is unique in that it can both motivate us to avoid or cause us to withdraw from the stimulus creating it. When we think about pain, all of us have a story to tell. Stop for a minute and think about a painful moment in your life—the death of a loved one, a breakup, stubbing your toe on your bed frame. Although these stimuli create a feeling of pain, we must remember that there is a reason our brains tell us there is pain. Without this, the ability to feel pain would not exist. This simple fact will be crucial to understanding how pain affects us as we continue onward.

Pain can be divided into both physical and emotional pain. Physical pain is defined as an unpleasant sensory experience associated with actual or potential tissue damage. Psychological pain is defined as an unpleasant subjective (perceived) experience characterized as an awareness of negative changes in the self and its functions. Although completely different, with each type there is an associated negative experience that can alter our ability to function normally, altering the quality of our lives. If a person breaks her leg, the ability to function in day-to-day activities can be severely hindered as mobility will be altered during that time. Likewise, the loss of a loved one can and usually will affect a person's ability to focus on the tasks at hand, thus crippling productivity or the desire to carry out usual daily tasks. While pain is something we all experience, how we react to pain or the intensity of it is based upon numerous factors. Societal norms, past experiences, beliefs, and degree of damage can affect our perception. However, in any given circumstance, our perception of pain can reveal to us something deeper as we traverse this life.

PHYSICAL PAIN

Pain is vital to survival. When an organism feels pain, it will pull away from the stimulus and protect the affected body part to maintain its life. Physical pain can be viewed as a "red flag" that something has gone wrong in the normal state of living. However, what happens when the brain gets confused? Can we feel physical pain even in the absence of a harmful stimulus?

The rubber hand illusion is a classic example of just how important the brain's perception is in dictating our experience of pain. The illusion was conducted by Italian researchers to show how the mind combines information from the senses to create feeling. Volunteers sat down with their forearms on the table. Their right arm was placed in a box and a lifelike rubber hand was placed in line with their shoulder. A tablecloth was placed over the box and covered the eyes' ability to see it and their real arm and hand. The researchers then stroked the real middle finger inside the box to light touch while at the same time doing the same thing to the rubber hand. After one to two minutes of stroking the real hand, the researchers stopped touching the real hand. Astonishingly, the volunteers continued to perceive touch when the rubber hand was stroked. Despite no actual physical feedback, the brain perceived the rubber hand as part of the body.[21]

This example displays the importance of our minds in the sensation of pain. The state of our mind will dictate how we perceive pain. When our minds are focused on the pain, although we may feel extreme discomfort, studies show that we heal faster and with fewer residual effects. It seems that recognizing pain has a way of healing us. However, if we try to forget about the pain by blocking it out or not acknowledging it, the pain does not seem to ever go away, as scar tissue and tissue impairment will ensue despite the body's healing mechanisms.

The invention of pain medication was a wonderful discovery in decreasing the body's perception of the pain felt. These medications work by either stopping the signal of pain from leaving the affected area or by blocking the signal in the brain. In the case of drugs classified as an opioid (Morphine, Oxycodone, Codeine), these medications bind to receptors in the brain, blocking the sensation of pain. When used for true physical pain from a noxious

---

21 Marieke Rhode, Luca Di Massimiliano, and Marc O Ernst, "The Rubber Hand Illusion: Feeling of Ownership and Proprioceptive Drift Do Not Go Hand in Hand," PLOS One, 6, no. 6, (June, 2011), https://www.doi.org/10.1371/journal.pone.0021659.

stimulus, these medications can significantly decrease your overall perception of the pain and help in aiding your recovery by allowing you to push past a point that you wouldn't have thought impossible. However, when these medications are used to treat psychological pain or chronic pain from no known injury, this can lead to dependence and addiction.

PSYCHOLOGICAL PAIN

This topic is tricky. There are many theories on what causes psychological pain. For the purposes of this book, I will write what makes the most sense to me. I know many trolls will come out from under the bridge to try and discredit me. For those who do, you need to remove the plank from your eye before pointing out the speck in mine. I will tread lightly on this topic because I do not want you to throw out the baby with the bathwater. I know this will hit home to some but to explain this chapter's hard fact, I must show the differences in pain.

The loss of a loved one can be classified as psychological pain. Verbal abuse can be classified as psychological pain. The absence of something you desire can lead to psychological pain. What do all these scenarios have in common? The definition of psychological pain is the answer. To put it another way, "the pain caused is the result of your awareness that a disruption has occurred in the way you view yourself, the way you live your life or the way you have a need met."

Emotional pain is a display that a need like love, autonomy, or acceptance has been disrupted. The balance of who we are and our purpose in life can be confusing at times. When we have the rug pulled out from under us, we will naturally challenge our existence if we do not ground ourselves on something greater than ourselves. Heartache, longing, or experiencing shame/embarrassment is natural at times in our lives. However, whether these experiences cause us psychological pain is determined by whether a deep need is met outside of the stimulus. A person who understands their purpose and who they are can endure these trials of life without the burden of long-lasting emotional pain. When we think about a stable person, I believe it is based upon them knowing their worth, their purpose, and their ability to see the bigger picture of their life. Unstable people have tendencies to run, stay locked in unhealthy situations, or fall into depression as they base their worthiness on factors outside of their control.

Each person has a limit to how much pain they can endure. The analogy I use to describe emotional health is that each one of us has a bucket of water. Some people have small buckets and others have large ones. Some people naturally have their buckets filled with water and others' buckets are fairly empty. Emotional distress occurs when the bucket of your life begins to overflow. This overflow manifests itself as an emotional reaction or psychiatric illness. Although this example is simple and non-inclusive, it helps illustrate why certain people can bounce back to a steady state faster than others after a negative experience. Regardless of who you are, we all have a breaking point of emotional turmoil, and when that happens depends on factors both internal and external. We must remember that each one of us is different. We learn about people in snapshots of time, and judgment is not for us to make.

> **IF WE WANT HELP, I BELIEVE THAT WE MUST IDENTIFY THE UNMET NEED, OR THE PROCESS WILL CONTINUE INDEFINITELY.**

Likewise, our brains have an innate capacity to handle only so much pain. Our brains constantly evaluate our surroundings based on our five senses and the scenarios we experience throughout our lives. Physical pain + emotional pain = total pain. If we have intense emotional pain, we can only process a small amount of physical pain and vice versa. This phenomenon explains why certain people can self-mutilate with little regard for the physical pain it is causing. This dangerous slope of trying to offload emotional pain for physical pain can be seen as a cry for help. If we want help, I believe that we must identify the unmet need, or the process will continue indefinitely.

PAIN LINGERS WITHOUT CONFRONTATION AND ACCEPTANCE

For most, suffering is an unnecessary time-waster. Although we each suffer to some degree, the classic saying: "Pain is inevitable, but the degree of suffering is optional" is a truly simple way of describing life. Suffering can be defined as the state of undergoing pain, distress, or hardship. As in previous chapters, a state is something that alters your mind. It moves past what we feel or experience and elevates us to a way of living. Suffering can be put into a formula:

Pain x Resistance = Suffering

When we look further into the formula, we can see that the degree to which we experience suffering is truly up to us. Let's apply this formula as an example.

John is upset that his wife spends too much money. He loves his wife and can't believe that this is happening to him. He works hard every day to provide for his family, but it seems his labors are in vain as he never makes ends meet. He tries to push down his emotions of anger, resentment, and sadness. Eventually, John feels he suffered long enough, and this results in him stepping away from his marriage.

John felt emotional pain, as most of us would. The pain he felt was created as he questioned his own existence and purpose of his life. I have heard many men and women state this exact thought. However, John rejected his emotions day after day, creating resistance. He refused to allow his emotions to "just be". This led to inner conflict, which multiplied his pain exponentially. His entire state of mind was altered because of this resistance, leading him to see no way out except to stop the pain. The thought of easing the resistance by healthily acknowledging his emotions eluded him. His suffering could have been avoided and the outcome of this scenario could have been drastically different. This is the key to suffering and pain. If you lower the resistance you place on the pain, you gain victory.

Unfortunately, most of us do the exact opposite and put up more resistance than we know. Many of us try to avoid the pain at all costs instead of accepting our current situation. The pain in our lives can be by our own doing or by someone else's doing. Regardless of the cause, we must accept our authentic selves. We must look at who we truly are and what we are struggling with.

Removal of the pain is just a part of the healing process. If I fell and broke my leg, I wouldn't get better if I fell again. Removal of the pain would be important but figuring out why I fell in the first place would be the most crucial to healing. We must accept our current reality despite how uncomfortable that might be. We must pay attention to our thoughts, feelings, and desires and be ready to articulate them if needed. Lastly, we must plan for a better future with the awareness that suffering is of our making. The absolute worst thing we can do is think we can outrun our pain by ignoring it, replacing it with something/someone that we feel will make us better in that moment, or thinking we can change the nature of what is hurting us. Every single one of those actions creates resistance, and the suffering we can experience has the potential to cause ripples in our lives for years to come.

YOU CAN'T RUN FROM WHAT'S INSIDE OF YOU

At some point in our lives, every one of us has tried to escape some lingering pain from our past. Whether it is the pain of childhood, the pain of a failed marriage, or the pain of a life experience, we have all tried to run. Although we think that escape is the only way out, this resistance seems to carry over into whatever endeavor we undertake next. As I have gotten older, I can look back and ponder on my pain, touch upon it, and push forward till I find breakthrough. When we finally decide to accept the pain, that is when it hurts the worst for a short while. However, this could elevate us to the next level of our walk. Let me repeat my opening verse that I will be building upon:

> "And the God of all grace, who called you to his eternal glory in Christ, after you have suffered a little while, will himself restore you and make you strong, firm, and steadfast." —1 Peter 5:10

When I read this Bible verse, I am reminded that suffering is part of life. It is necessary because it reveals our character so that we can cut away those things that hold us back. Running from pain and creating suffering is a sure way of dragging this process on. By running and not confronting, we delay our transformation into a position of strength and the pain of our actions becomes more and more intense.

Before discussing my own experience with this hard lesson, you must understand that I thought I was smart enough to outrun my past. I thought I could thrive in avoiding what was hurting me. I thought I could stay within a safe zone and that pain would not find me. Nothing could be further from the truth, and I am grateful that eventually, I stopped running. I only wish I had learned this lesson sooner.

By now, you know the kind of life I was living. I would bounce from one relationship to another. I would seek pleasure to numb the pain hidden deep within me. The pain was from rejection. Rejection is something we all have felt. Being picked last in gym class, being left for someone else, or being passed over for a promotion are all examples of rejection experiences that lead us to question our self-worth. For me, rejection started early in life and continued until I was ready to face the facts. The symptoms of my rejection led to unstable attachments, exaggerating my accomplishments, and constant worry about whether I was liked in all situations. Little did I know that I would carry this rejection into every new relationship and job I started.

In my own journey, the first part of healing took place when I realized that I was running. Just like with any addiction or problem, acknowledgment has a unique effect. It brings the problem to the forefront of our minds. If we do not know what we are battling inside, how can we expect to defeat it? This came to me after a string of bad relationships. I was living my best life, or so I thought. I had obtained positions of influence in my work, and I was answering numerous texts from women daily. However, in the quiet moments of life, when I would wake up and then relax at night, I felt empty. I felt alone, like I was just drifting. Despite an outward appearance of success, I could not shake the despair I was feeling. It was in those moments that the whisper of rejection became a scream. I was not getting closer to a deeper level of intimacy with anyone. When I found myself getting close to someone, I would look for ways to sabotage the relationship. I would text others and arrange for meetings, and the cycle would repeat. I discovered after years of this, with no true healthy relationship, that I was trying to escape the pain of rejection.

The greatest damage that rejection causes is self-inflicted. Just when we are hurting the most, we go and damage it further. I began to realize that I was causing the pain in my life. I was projecting this pain onto others which, in turn, was causing them to feel rejection. It had become a vicious cycle of inflicting damage on my self-esteem. My defensive instinct was to run, but I finally decided to face the pain of my rejection.

> # I HAD DETERMINED THAT THOSE WHO DID NOT SEE ME FOR WHO I WANTED TO BE HAD TO GO.

Now, I can't tell you that this was easy. First, I had to find true value in myself. For me, this came in the form of believing that I was not who I had been. This is difficult when those all around you know you as someone else. I would venture to say that 90 percent of people tried sticking me back into the box of who I was. I had determined that those who did not see me for who I wanted to be had to go. I began cutting people out of my life one person at a time. Let me tell you, this process is harder than you think. I had to cut people out whom I had known for years, but when you are stuck gaining your self-worth from others, it is necessary to purposefully cut those people out if you want to grow. Next, I had to discover my true purpose in life. I will discuss this more in the next chapter. Third, I had to start living a life that was congruent with who I wanted and was supposed to be. Life began to look a lot different, and plenty of naysayers said it would not last. Like Job, I could not listen to my friends or family; this journey was my own to complete and nobody could do it for me.

As the changes went on, I found that I could speak about my past mistakes with authority. I found that I was letting the past go from all the hurt I experienced, and I forgave myself for the wrongs I had done. My resistance to rejection grew smaller and my suffering began to vanish. Transformation was taking place as my character was refining, and a hope of a better tomorrow began to take hold. The pain that I felt dealing with the rejection began to fade, and now, it is just a scar from the life I once lived. Although my rejection pain faded, the scar is a constant reminder of how far I have come. I think back on past relationships and sometimes wonder about what could have been. In the quiet of the night, I remember the pain I caused others because of my inability to face the pain of my rejection sooner. Then, my mind begins to stray elsewhere as I realize that although I have suffered, I am being restored and coming back stronger, more stable, and more committed to living a life that is honorable and purposeful. This is a comforting thought.

> IF YOU CONTINUE TO DIVE DEEP, TOUCH ON THE PAIN, AND ARE COMMITTED TO HEALING, ANYTHING IS POSSIBLE.

In your own journey, remember that confrontation is the key to lowering resistance to your pain. You are going to suffer and that is unavoidable. Some of you may need a therapist to help you unpack your pain and your resistance points. Asking for help is likely necessary as the pain has been masked by years of defense mechanisms. Therapy such as EMDR or behavioral alterations may be crucial to get you to where you can face the pain. I sought therapy for years before I realized the true nature of my failed relationships. These therapists helped bring to light what was inside of me, although I could not see the root of the problem initially. If you continue to dive deep, touch on the pain, and are committed to healing, anything is possible. During this process, you will find that your mind will begin to change. You will find that your perception of pain changes and what once hurt immensely becomes more like an ache. Breakups or deaths that challenge your very existence will still happen, but suffering can be minimal or even avoided. It's time to rip the band-aid off despite the intense pain you will feel once you identify the source. Whatever pain you feel now will ultimately render any future pain obsolete, and your future self and relationships will thank you.

HARD TRUTH #8:
LEARN YOUR PURPOSE AND TRUE NATURE.
And Resist the Voices of Outside Influences.

If it bears fruit next year fine! If not, cut it down.
Luke 13:9

Purpose is the why that explains your existence. Without purpose, your existence has no meaning. Likewise, without purpose, there is no passion to pursue something greater than your own selfish ambitions, because you will have no self-control, boundaries, or convictions. Your Creator has given you a purpose—a unique set of talents, skills, and gifts that enable you to truly succeed in life. The problem with purpose is that no one can achieve it for you. Regardless of your social stature, wealth, or accolades, the nature of purpose is a self-journey that only you can discover. Your mission, if you choose to accept it, is to strive to be who you were born to be. This mission is critical to moving forward from whatever you are facing now, will keep you from backsliding, and will sustain you in the toughest of times.

In 1415, during the Battle of Agincourt, the English morale was low as they faced the overwhelming force of the French. Knowing this, Henry V, the commander of the English forces rallied his men by appealing to their sense of honor and purpose to a cause greater than themselves. Although this purpose is more generalized rather than personal, the point is abundantly clear. William Shakespeare writes:

"If we are mark'd to die, we are enough
To do our country loss; and if to live,
The fewer men, the greater share of honour...
Then will he strip his sleeve and show his scars,
And say "These wounds I had on Crispin's day."
Old men forget; yet all shall be forgot,
But he'll remember, with advantages,
What feats he did that day...
We few, we happy few, we band of brothers;
For he to-day that sheds his blood with me
Shall be my brother; be he never so vile,
This day shall gentile his condition;
And gentlemen in England now-a-bed
Shall think themselves accursed they were not here,
And hold their manhood cheap while any speaks
That fought with us upon Saint Crispin's day."[22]

There are very few who will truly discover their purpose in life. They will drift from one thing to another trying to find satisfaction throughout their days. Some will jump from woman to woman, some job to job, and others will stay lukewarm in their

---

22 William Shakespeare, "The St. Crispin's Day speech from Henry V," The Poetry Society, https://poetrysociety.org.uk/poems/the-st-crispins-day-speech-from-henry-v/.

pursuit to live a godly life. As the speech above states, those who find purpose will achieve honor. The scars of life will be apparent in the process, but they will never forget what brought them to the point where they are now. By seeking purpose, they will become who they were created to be by abandoning recklessness and succeeding in life. Those around them will want what they have but unless they are willing to go to battle, their purpose will not be found. Until you are willing to fight for the "why you were created?" there can be no "what can I do?" (your potential) or "where am I going?" (your destiny).

WHAT PURPOSE IS NOT

A disease has disrupted the world. I am not talking about the COVID-19 disease. I am referring to the belief that humans are trying to find meaning and not purpose in this world. Although these words may seem similar, the definitions of the two are very different and achieve two very different results.

Purpose is defined as *"the reason for which something is done or created or for which something exists."* When we look closely at this definition, one word stands out amongst all the others. Did you see it? The word CREATED implies something very powerful. It applies that there must be a creator. This means there has to be a blueprint for the creation, instructions on how to operate the creation, and guidelines for how to utilize the creation.

Let us try something: Reach into your pocket and pull out your phone. What do you see? Do you see the freedom to harness or obtain knowledge on anything you want to know? Do you see an object that has linked you to the world at all hours of the day? Do you see it as a way to communicate? Do you see it as a way to strike a nail into a piece of wood? Why wouldn't you? The phone is a hard object that can easily hammer the nail into place. So why not use it as a hammer? Well, the phone was not created for this purpose. Let's assume the phone was happy that it was being used for this task. Sure, you could use it for that purpose, but what would happen? The phone would likely no longer be able to operate in the original purpose it was created for. It would not be happy for very long if it couldn't even be used! This is what separates purpose from meaning.

Meaning is defined as *"intended to convey, signify, or intend a particular thing or notion."* Another definition is *"have as a motive or excuse in explanation."* Meaning is the emotional significance of why we do what we do. Meaning doesn't just exist on its own, it's something we create and feel. Our emotions and the lessons we learn throughout life can constantly change our search for meaning. It is a forever-moving goalpost with the potential to change daily. Let's say I decided to search for my life's meaning. If I base meaning off its definition, then I am trying to convey to myself and others my existence in this world. If I did not sleep the night before, if I didn't eat breakfast, or if I read a negative review about the way I practiced healthcare and used these external influences to determine the meaning of my life, I would find it pretty difficult to find. Pursuing meaning is a dead end for the discovery of existence.

As you can see, there is a vast difference between meaning and purpose. Meaning is dictated by the world around us. It can change with the weather and can isolate us on an island where my life is my own. There is no reason to exist except to obtain joy and happiness for what I believe works for me. Although you might find joy in helping starving children or saving stray dogs, your life will be locked into a cycle of explanation. To put it another way, meaning grants me the grace to live in this world by chance. If I search for meaning, I have no accountability to a Creator, and this, my friend, leads us on a dangerous path of ultimate self-destruction via a perceived fulfillment of what living truly means based upon the secular or New Age philosophy of the day.

On the other hand, purpose is something placed inside of us by a Creator. It serves a cause greater than us, greater than your country, and greater than the world. It serves as the reason for your existence at this particular time in history. It is something that is unbridled by the world around you and is free of emotional constructs. There is no changing your purpose regardless of how hard you try. To search for purpose is a key to true fulfillment in life.

BENEFITS OF PURPOSE

Over the years, I have learned that without purpose, there can be no victory. With defeat after defeat throughout my life, it wasn't until I found my purpose that I could overcome my lusts, arrogance, and selfishness. It was not found in relationships, prayers focused on the problems, or seeking counselors to help me navigate my emotions and thoughts. Victory has become possible because I have sought my purpose. Without it, I would have fallen back into the same pits I had always fallen into before. Knowing your purpose has many benefits. Purpose can give you confidence that you are on the right path. Purpose can give you a perspective that allows you to see through the crap of life. It allows you to see past your immediate hardships and dangers. Purpose can give you satisfaction as you journey toward an objective goal. Although your path may twist and turn, you know there is something greater in the end. However, of all that purpose can give, the greatest is perseverance.

I have written two-thirds of this book. Through sharing my stories, I have re-lived my life and gained strength from it daily. I have been focused on providing insight so that others would not fall into the same traps. Just when I thought I had finished the hardest parts, I decided to take a well-needed break from writing. I had come so far and had aired out my dirty laundry for others to see. I knew I was doing what was asked of me and felt comfortable (not arrogant or assured) that I could withstand the attacks that I assumed would come my way as I learned and healed more than I ever have.

> **IT WAS THE PERSEVERANCE FOUND IN PURPOSE THAT KEPT ME STANDING.**

It was an extremely busy time in my life. I was moving, work had become out of control as many of my projects were progressing from the planning stage to the execution stage at the same time. Morning after morning, I would find myself spending less and less time with God. I slept later, was meeting certain people who began encouraging my sinful embers and I was spending a lot of time surfing Netflix as I collapsed in my bed at night, not tired, but not motivated to do anything. I was falling again, slowly, but the writing was on the wall. I told myself it was just one day here and there, and I was using every excuse I could. I was doing nothing wrong compared to where I had come from but inside, I felt a strong conviction, and it did not come from pious prayer time or encouragement from friends. It came from something deeper that I had not known the previous times I had fallen backward. I had learned my purpose. I had reconnected to my Creator, and He was guiding me. It was the perseverance found in purpose that kept me standing. The purpose God had placed inside of me was bigger, bolder, and stronger than anything the world had to offer. It was bigger than my emotions. It was bigger than my sexual desires. It was bigger than my ego. It was the turning point in my walk toward spiritual maturity. As 1 John 2:12-14 says:

> *I am writing to you, dear children, because your sins have been forgiven on account of his name. I am writing to you, fathers, because you know him who is from the beginning. I am writing to you, young men, because you have overcome the evil one.*

Up until this time, I was a young man. I was able to withstand the evil one but that could not last without maturity. I would have had to lean on others to help me withstand the attacks just like my teenage sons look to me for protection and help with certain projects. Moving to the next level and having the ability to stand alone, if necessary, can only be accomplished by "knowing" your Creator through understanding your purpose.

DANGERS OF KNOWING YOUR PURPOSE

You didn't think it would be that easy, did you? Although learning your purpose will sustain you through difficult times, you have to be careful—knowing your purpose does create difficult times. I have recognized four dangers, four destroyers, four horsemen of purpose destruction. I have witnessed these at work in my own life, and to spare you time in figuring out where you may go wrong, just remember D-A-R-C.

D–Deception: You look to others or push your own agenda.

A–Arrogance: You believe you know, without confirmation or instruction, how and when your purpose will be used.

R–Reverence: You focus more on the journey over the Creator.

C–Criticism: You believe you know better, and your purpose is greater than another's.

Deception

Deception is the act of persuading someone to accept as truth what is false. All throughout history, people have studied ways to deceive others, and some have become quite good. In fact, entire books have been devoted to deception such as *The Art of War*[23] or *The Screwtape Letters*.[24] These books open the door for us to see how subtle deception can be for achieving an unseen goal. Likewise, when we allow ourselves to blame others for why our purpose is not manifesting, we convince ourselves that others are holding us back. Similarly, deception can take place when we look to others to show us the way instead of allowing God to guide us. Once deception occurs, we tend to open ourselves up to shortcuts. When you pursue a shortcut, you will find yourself starting over again in your pursuit of purpose. Deception can destroy purpose. Understand that purpose is a journey and seeking the path of

---

23   Sun Tzu, The Art of War (Minneapolis, MN: Filiquarian, 2007).
24   C.S. Lewis, Screwtape Letters (San Francisco, CA: HarperOne, 2015).

least resistance is not always the best course of action if you find yourself struggling to succeed.

Arrogance

Arrogance is an attitude of superiority or self-importance. When you learn your purpose, there is a tendency to fall back into an "I know better" attitude pattern. Should you do this, you will begin making assumptions about how your purpose should work. Examples can be found all over. Let's say you believe your purpose is to speak to large crowds on a topic you have experience in. You seek out a person of importance with influence to help you achieve this goal. Instead of waiting, learning, refining, and speaking in front of smaller groups to start, you go straight to a large crowd. In doing this, the possibility of failing is very likely. You "jumped the gun" on your purpose by thinking you knew exactly how you would succeed. This is arrogance, and arrogance can destroy purpose, even if your intentions are wholesome. Wait for the right timing and you can avoid arrogance.

Reverence

Reverence is a deep respect for someone or something. The trap of focusing more on your journey than your Creator can lead to stagnation. Although you may find yourself appreciative of how far you have come, you must always remember that the journey was laid out from the beginning. You were meant to be on this particular journey. You are not any better than the next person for having walked it. Reverence for anything other than your Creator destroys purpose. Pay attention to your own natural tendencies to find glory in the walk you are on and refocus on what really matters and why you are on the journey to begin with.

Criticism

Criticism is the act of making judgments based on perceived faults or mistakes. As humans, it appears natural to criticize others. For example, I often remind myself that anyone can have a bad day. This is especially true when I engage in a negative conversation or encounter. My natural tendency would be to label that person as an asshole. However, I try, not always successfully, to think about what may have led to this negative experience. Sure, it would be very easy to label someone as unfriendly or unsympathetic, but what don't I know? Perhaps they fought with their spouse before leaving the house. Maybe they found out their mother was diagnosed with cancer. Whatever the scenario, I must remember that the course of events that took place before our encounter had nothing to do with me. The animosity or argumentative conversation that I experienced is a byproduct of something other than me. I must be slower to criticize someone when I don't know all the facts. Likewise, I must remember that my purpose is mine alone. There is nothing greater about mine than the next person's. The events that led to someone else's revelation of their purpose will most likely remain unknown to you. Criticism suggests that your purpose is more important than another, and this attitude will hinder your ability to succeed. You must stay humble and remember that you meet people in a snippet of time in their lives. Stay focused on your own pursuit, and you will avoid making judgments on what you do not know about someone else. In a nutshell, stop comparing yourself to others.

LEARNING PURPOSE

I wish I could say that I have some groundbreaking method for learning your purpose. I am not going to give you a foundational "follow these steps to freedom". If there was such a formula, I am sure someone a lot smarter than me would have discovered it by now. Sure, others may have the answer and go around teaching all about it. However, you must remember that their path worked for them but may not work for you. Do not compare yourself to them, as this will be your tendency. Do not lose faith in your own journey if all you have heard doesn't work for you. Purpose can only be achieved by your relentless pursuit of it, and how you get there is your own voyage. I told you at the beginning of the book that I am not revealing any new information that hasn't been revealed before. What I am doing is speaking from personal experience. I am throwing my hat in the ring and expanding this conversation. This is what worked for me and perhaps may steer you in a direction that you have never been before. Let's begin. . . .

Who Are You Alone in the Quiet of the Night?

The answer to this question focuses on your natural abilities. You get to let go of the façade and wipe the fake smile off your face and just be you. This is important because it allows you to reconnect to yourself. You do not have to listen to the world around you that tells you who they think you are. The first part of your journey is finding peace within yourself and understanding how you were made. This is not an "accept yourself for who you are" pep talk, but simply, "If you could do anything, for yourself only, what would you do?" The answer to this question may surprise you.

I found myself asking this question over and over again. It usually followed a bad date or a fight with someone. I would ask myself this question even while disconnecting from the world while playing Xbox after a long day of work. I was unknowingly placing myself in a position that silenced the world around me. I quieted the voices around me and just became me. The breakthrough happened one night while jamming to "Paint it, Black" by the Rolling Stones[25] on Guitar Hero, of all things.

> I BELIEVE THAT MOST PEOPLE WHO SAY THEY ARE JUST LOOKING FOR CLOSURE ARE, IN FACT, LOOKING FOR VALIDATION THAT THEY MADE THE RIGHT DECISION.

Once you have discovered who you are, you have to accept the mistakes of your past and the problems in your present situation.

You can only blame yourself for the situation you are in. You are the only one who walks in your shoes. I agree that many will influence your life, but ultimately, the decision of how you live it rests upon you. Anything good or bad falls on you. Be careful to avoid the people who keep trying to tell you how you should feel. Beware of the people who are looking for closure that somehow you can miraculously give. Closure happens when you

---

[25] Rolling Stones, vocalists, "Paint it, Black," by Mick Jagger and Keith Richards, released May 7, 1966, track 1 on Aftermath, London Records.

have accepted something for how it is. No person can help you with that. I believe that most people who say they are just looking for closure are, in fact, looking for validation that they made the right decision.

Explore Your Thoughts and Play Them Out.
Thoughts can be exciting. They can transport you to another place but can also guide you in the direction you should go. When you begin to think about your thoughts, it's like being in a virtual playground. You can play out scenario after scenario without having to live with a consequence. Thoughts are powerful as you dissect and look at all angles to find the best possibility. In the movie, Avengers: Infinity War, a gut-wrenching scene takes place between Dr. Strange and Tony Stark that explains this best:

Dr. Strange: "I looked forward in time. I saw 14,000,605 futures."

Tony Stark: "In how many of those futures do the Avengers defeat Thanos?"

Strange: "One."[26]

God knows the one thought or path that you should take to achieve fulfillment in life. Although it is fun to play around with thoughts, be careful about what path the decisions you make are taking you. Focus on finding your moral compass and let that dictate your direction. When you find that compass, you can begin to reconnect to the source of your purpose.

---

26 Anthony Russo and Joe Russo, Avengers: Infinity War (April 23, 2018; Burbank, CA: Marvel Studios), Dolby Theatre.

Reconnect with God.

God meets us all in different places. For some of us, it requires travel into the wilderness. For others, God meets us while we cut the grass or fold laundry. Just remember that God knows exactly where you will be able to receive His attention. What works for someone may not work for others. It took me going away for a month, growing a beard, and disconnecting from the world by quieting my cell phone and just listening to nothing. That nothing ended up becoming everything as God met me, showed me the way back, and reminded me of the gifts He gave me to achieve my purpose.

Be gentle with yourself when you go back since it's not always easy to let go of old identities or interests.

The hardest critic you have is yourself. When we make a mistake (and you will), try to let go of the failure mentality. Look for your wins up to the point of failure, realize where you went wrong by retracing the steps, and forgive yourself while you evaluate how to get better the next time.

Keep Moving Forward One Day at a Time.

Time will always move forward. The richest, strongest, or smartest person can never have more time than what they are given. Unfortunately, the lifestyle we choose to live can shorten our allotted time. Some would say that "you only live once." If I chose to live that way, the immediate itch would be scratched, but what about the next day? Can I still scratch that itch with the decision I made yesterday?

Although it is true that you only live once, you have to decide how and why you are going to live. You can choose to feed every pleasure you can afford, or you can practice self-restraint to live for something greater than yourself. You can choose to blame others for your failures, or you can look within yourself to find forgiveness and move forward. The ability to look to your life and remove what is not helping you grow is the key to purposeful success. When you learn to let go of three things—others' opinions of you, the way you thought life was going to go, or the belief that you are indefinitely locked into your past—an amazing thing happens. You begin to believe that only your and God's acceptance of yourself is important. Once you have achieved that, purpose will drive you forward, and it is amazing what you will leave behind as you pursue it.

CONCLUSION

Purpose is the why that explains your existence. Once you learn your purpose, you are in a unique position of control—you are less influenced by those around you. You can look at those who slander you and say, "That is not me," and actually believe it. You have a sense of determination that will sustain you in the darkest of times, and I can promise you that those dark times will come. You will gain the ability to see the fruit of your works for what they are. You will be able to see other people's agendas toward your life and how you were so easily influenced in the past. Finding purpose is taking the black hood off your head and seeing the world for what it is. It's time to stop filling your life with trinkets of insignificance that only deter you or cloud your mind. It's time to stop putting what the world tells you that you need into your life. It's time to stop letting your transient desires and emotions dictate your decisions. It's time to take the journey of discovering your true purpose.

This journey is not easy, but I can say, with certainty, that it is the one thing that will last indefinitely. The lasting effect of purpose is possible in true transformation and not just change. This transformation into the best version of ourselves is what we all are trying to seek, but few of us ever find.

HARD TRUTH #9:
REJECT THE LABELS AND DARE TO SPEAK YOUR TRUTH.

"I looked for someone among them who would build up the wall and stand before me in the gap on behalf of the land so I would not have to destroy it, but I found no one."
Ezekiel 22:30

"You live within a world of hate." I will never forget the date who told me this. I was sitting at the table enjoying my cannoli when this hit me like a ton of bricks. I was sharing my thoughts on a particular subject and before I knew it, I was sitting there speechless and questioning my own reality. Something happens to you when your reality of what you hold true is questioned.

Some erupt in a spew of profanity, and a yelling match would pursue. Some organize protests and look for likeminded individuals to justify their feelings. Others blow off the perceived ignorance and just shake it off. Others would throw a drink at the person across from them. However, there are some who look within themselves. They take the negative experience to figure out if the statement made about them was true and why. This statement led me on a search for the true meaning of hate and an honest exploration of whether I was holding any hate within *my* heart. If I did, I needed to find where it was rooted and pull it out. If I didn't, then I needed to search for the cause of the claim. What started as a good date ended as a frustrating one, but finished with self-reflection that altered my outlook and removed a deep block that was holding me back. To tell this story well, I need to define and separate hate from righteous hate.

WHAT IS HATE?

Hate is defined as intense hostility and aversion, usually derived from fear, anger, or a sense of injury. Like many other words in this book, hate conveys something deeper than an emotion. Hate is a state of mind that can define your character or dictate your actions by involving choices or behaviors. This is important to understand as hate is the bridge from your emotions to action. Hate truly is a catalyst for many of the things that are wrong in this world. The fear and anger that fuel hate are based on selfish motives or entitlement. Hate is usually associated with envy when you consider something unfair that someone else has what you lack. This type of hate hurts people because of the response it will produce in those it is directed toward. The response is usually one of retaliation, isolation, or division.

On the contrary, righteous hate is one that cares about others and the path they are on that will bring harm. It attacks a problem and not the person portraying the problem. It seeks to bring about redemptive action to make the wrong right. It is hate for something that, if corrected, would make the world a better place. This kind of hate is drastically different compared to hate as defined by the world.

Throughout the Bible, the word hate is mentioned numerous times and distinguishes between righteous and unrighteous hate. Proverbs 6:16-19 (ESV) writes,

There are six things that the Lord hates, seven that are an abomination to him: haughty eyes, a lying tongue, and hands that shed innocent blood, a heart that devises wicked plans, feet that make haste to run to evil, a false witness who breathes out lies, and one who sows discord among brothers.

However, John 3:20 (ESV) states,

"For everyone who does wicked things hates the light and does not come to the light, lest his works should be exposed."

> HOWEVER, ATTRIBUTING ALL HATE AS A NEGATIVE THING IS BELITTLING AND, QUITE FRANKLY, DISMISSIVE.

The difference between the two types of hate is painfully obvious. Righteous hate is hate directed toward things that causes pain and suffering to others. Unrighteous hate exposes a person's state of mind toward others and can reveal the character of a person's heart by how he or she views or acts towards a person or group of people. Unrighteous hate has existed for selfish or prideful reasons for millennia and has caused so much pain in this world. It is easy to see how most people accept any display of hate as a bad thing. However, attributing all hate as a negative thing is belittling and, quite frankly, dismissive. If something is just flat-out wrong, it is okay to hate the wrong but be careful that the hate you express is not focused on the person doing the wrong. As a matter of fact, now that I think about it, my date was right—I do live with hate but not for the reasons she accused me of.

WHAT I HATE . . .

Some people hate spiders. Some people hate lines at Starbucks. Some people hate mayonnaise. The list of things "we hate" can go on indefinitely. By using the expression "I hate," we have watered down the true meaning of the word. As I explained above, hate is a state of mind. Sure, you might have a fear of spiders that might alter your perception of them, but could you say that you are angry with them? If you aren't angry with them, then can you really hate them? Meaning, does your thoughts about them lead to true retaliation, isolation, or division?

When I think about things I hate, three very distinct things come to mind. I know that people may or may not agree with what I am about to say. I know that people may find offense if their jobs, careers, or belief system revolves around these three things, but I would not be holding to what I believe if I were dishonest about how I felt. The three things I abhor are:

1) Making money off another's sinful nature.
AND
2) Preying on the weak in a time of crisis.
AND

3) Categorizing someone and imposing personal bias based upon something unchangeable.

The hate I have for these three things is not only rooted in my own experience, but I can back these up from scripture. I have heard people defend their stance against my hate for these things to justify their means of personal gain. In fact, just a few weeks ago, I was told (close to accurate), "I was jealous that I spent a decade of my time in school to make less money than someone who spent no time in college. You are the idiot who has no thoughts on business because this country was built by entrepreneurs. You just hate that someone was smarter than you and figured out how to make money. They are just trying to make a living." Now mind you, this discussion was over someone who made a living selling, distributing, and profiting off gambling tools. I want to be clear on something, I never once said I hated the person. I was very clear that I did not agree with *how* they made their money. However, like most things, people hear what they want to hear. So let me break down each of my hates:

Making Money Off Another's Sinful Behavior

"I found a niche to make money."

Matthew 18:7 (NLV) says, *"It is bad for the world because of that which makes people sin. Men will be tempted to sin. But it is bad for the one who is the reason for someone to sin."*

In the fourth century AD, a Christian Monk named Evagrius Ponticus classified the seven deadly sins. Although they closely follow Proverbs 6:16-19 (shown earlier in the chapter), this list simplified sin into seven distinct words:

1) Pride (Vanity)
2) Greed
3) Wrath
4) Envy
5) Lust
6) Gluttony
7) Sloth

Look at those who have the most influence in this world. Look to any profession, career, or job and see who seems to make the most money. It is usually the person who targets another person's natural tendency or passion, exploits it and does it well.

I have lived in many places. In fact, I have moved over twenty times throughout my life. In each place I have lived as an adult, one thing has remained true. The largest house in the neighborhood is always the entrepreneur with questionable business practices. In one place, the largest house was owned by an online porn mogul (Lust). In another, the largest house was owned by the alcohol license distributor (Gluttony). In another, the largest house was owned by the plastic surgeon who only did cosmetic surgery (Pride). He once told me, "Cleft lips, burn grafting, or facial deformities don't make me any money". It seems the formula to make money is very easy. Although this does include tapping into the entrepreneurial spirit that "built this country", we must ask at what cost.

On the contrary, do you think your local teacher lives in the house on the ocean from her career alone? How about your local paramedic? Think he drives that Porsche from his third twenty-four-hour shift this week? How about your pastor? Think he flies first class to the South Pacific quarterly to his vacation house on his church's weekly tithes that pay his salary?

Public servants, healers, educators, farmers, soldiers, and church leaders pursue their careers usually for the desire to help others. One thing I have heard murmured and argued over relentlessly is why some church leaders are "hated on" because they live in a nice house. I would think the reverse would be true. We should be happy that they have found success in their careers as long as the success came in an honorable way. An honorable pastor with book deals, public speaking engagements, and a podcast should do well in life both spiritually and financially. The hate felt toward them would be classified as unrighteous and is usually bred from envy or selfishness. Solution: We should be highlighting these success stories. We should be showing people that success can be found in public service or in helping others despite what the world would have you believe. Just because you serve poor people doesn't mean you have to share their fortune.

To sum it up, look to yourself before you judge another. Do you feel anger that advances toward hate because an injustice has been done or do you feel you deserve what you do not have that someone else does? Most of the time, I do not believe people are even conscious of their career choices and are respectable people making a living. Remember, it is not the person but the practice of exploiting another's inequity that I hate. I hate it for what it symbolizes. I hate how it can keep people in bondage. I hate how it has the potential to bring out the very worst in people.

Preying on the Weak in a Time of Crisis

"There is a hurricane coming, and I am selling a $2 bottle of water for $100 dollars...."

Nehemiah 5:6-8:

> When I heard their outcry and these charges, I was very angry. I pondered them in my mind and then accused the nobles and officials. I told them, "You are charging your own people interest!" So I called together a large meeting to deal with them and said: "As far as possible, we have bought back our fellow Jews who were sold to the Gentiles. Now you are selling your own people, only for them to be sold back to us!"

We have all heard stories of price gouging. Price gouging is defined as "taking advantage of spikes in demand by charging exorbitant prices for necessities, often after a natural disaster or other state of emergency." For those who don't agree with me, I understand that the most common argument is supply and demand. I think the key for me is "exorbitant price on a necessity."

Supply and demand would dictate that a healthcare worker should be paid more in a time of crisis—agreed—but should they be paid more than those who assume more risk and are ultimately responsible for a patient just because they can? I have heard stories of individuals making over 500 percent more money to serve in a critically understaffed area. Is this fair? Some would say, "Good for those workers doing something to show their true value." Others would say, "Yah! Stick it to the CEOs and the Executive Board." Others would say, "I am finally getting what I am worth." If that was the case, why did you go into the field to begin with? You knew what you were signing up for and suddenly you are worth 500 percent more than you were the year before? Perhaps you are, and I will not argue that; but I ask the question: at what cost when it comes so quickly and forcefully? When your fellow healthcare workers get laid off because they are not in a "critical" job, is it worth it? When advancement into healthcare shortage areas has to stop to pay your salary, who does that benefit? That is price gouging on a grand scale and that is something I hate.

The reason I hate exorbitant price gouging is that it takes advantage of others and there is nothing they can do about it lawfully in that moment. Sure, we can loot and riot or we can steal in the immediate. Hell, in the days that follow, we can even orate awe-inspiring speeches but what can we really do at that moment? I believe that it is at that moment that the freedom to choose ceases. If I need water, then I will have to get water. If I can't afford water despite planning to buy water at one price but it has gone up 500 percent in a day, I am in a weakened position. I understand life is not always fair but when you are accustomed to a necessity for survival and access to that is immediately removed by a price tag much greater than before the crisis, that is what I hate.

Categorizing Someone and Imposing Personal Bias Based upon Something Unchangeable.

> Romans 15:7: "Accept one another, then,
> just as Christ accepted you."

If you are alive, you have experienced bias towards you. It does not matter your height, weight, skin color, accent, gender, belief system, brand of car, number of bedrooms in your house, how many kids you have, career, favorite sports team, and the list goes on and on. Bias is found everywhere and at least once every day you will experience it. Now, you may not know this directly, as someone may not express their thoughts about you to you, but it exists. Some things are of your own making and others are unchangeable.

Throughout our lives, we will change many things we believe in and what we stand for. These changes can come in many different ways. First, they may come when we choose to change a circumstance in our life. For example, a person may choose to change political affiliation when they land their first job. Likewise, a person may choose to live a different way based upon becoming married or starting a family than how they lived when single. Second, the changes may come as they are forced upon us. An example of this is when we get fired from a job or the death of a loved one from unforeseen circumstances. Lastly, what we believe may change when we look within ourselves or have an encounter that shakes the foundation of what we thought life meant. An example of this is becoming saved through Jesus Christ. You realize that parts of your life cannot go on as they were before you established this relationship. The common thread of all this is that as circumstances of life change, so does your thinking. We open ourselves up to certain biases from people who have not had our experiences and do not share our thoughts. You know what? That is okay. Sure, it may be frustrating at times, but this in itself is expected. Life would be boring if we were all carbon copies of one another. However, each one of the aforementioned phenomena is our choice. We made a conscious decision to believe something. The belief we have defines us to the world and to group ourselves with like-minded individuals is natural and encouraged. What I find abhorrent is the bias toward something you cannot change that is supposed to define who you are.

Grab your phone, turn on the TV, or walk around where you live. At every turn, you will see a bias toward something that is not based on your choice or life experience. The bias is based on how you were born. To simplify it, it is a bias toward your DNA. In society today, people prey on these differences. It enables them to commit crimes thinking someone is somehow less than them. It enables behaviors that destroy the fabric of a civilized society where there should be protection for the pursuit of happiness. It enables a mindset that allows an entitled attitude. Whether righteous in its cause or from a place of anger, to impose a bias on anyone based on something unchangeable or on outward appearance from birth is something I hate.

Hate is very real.

As the years go on throughout life, you will find that there are things that you hate. Life is not all unicorns and rainbows. However, I challenge you to ask yourself three questions about the thing you hate.

1) Does the hate come from a sense of entitlement?
2) Does the hate come from years of ignorance and conditioning?
3) Does the hate cause me to disrespect someone just because they may think or look differently than me?

If the answer to any of these questions is YES, then you may need to take a deeper look within yourself. Try to root out the reason for your hate. You may not like what you find, but hey, this may be the very thing holding you back from the life you always wanted.

CONCLUSION

At some point in your life, you will have multiple opportunities to stand up for what you value and declare your truth. I do believe that there is a time and a place to not be vulgar or obscene. Your truth is your truth. Nobody should have the right to silence you if they do not like what you have to say. One of my favorite quotes comes from Clinical Psychologist Jordan Peterson. He states, "In order to be able to think, you have to risk being offensive."[27] I promise you will offend someone. With everything you say and do, there is someone who will not like it.

> SOMEONE WILL MOST LIKELY HATE YOU BUT IF YOU AREN'T HATED, I ASK THE QUESTION, DO YOU REALLY STAND FOR ANYTHING AT ALL?

Why are we so afraid to stand up for what we believe? You can do your best to walk the eggshell path and please everyone but that will lead to a life of confusion and unfulfillment. You'll be so busy jumping from appeasing group after group and using the proper identifying word of the day that little time will be left for actually

---

27 Jordan Peterson, "In order to be able to think, you have to risk being offensive," Goodreads, https://www.goodreads.com/quotes/9235800-in-order-to-be-able-to-think-you-have-to.

making a difference in this world. Find your truth in this world and have the guts to stand for it. Someone will most likely hate you but if you aren't hated, I ask the question, do you really stand for anything at all? Remember to be respectful toward everyone as each person is on their own journey. Have the courage to speak out against what you believe but do it with an open ear to listen to others and maybe—just maybe—the pendulum of differences in society will swing to the middle, allowing for constructive and courteous debate on the issues plaguing the world.

HARD TRUTH #10:
PEOPLE WILL ALWAYS WATCH YOU.

"He will not shout or cry out, or raise his voice in the streets. . . . I, the Lord, have called you in righteousness; I will take hold of your hand. I will keep you and will make you to be a covenant for the people and a light for the Gentiles, to open the eyes that are blind, to free the captives from prison and to release from the dungeon those who sit in darkness."
Isaiah 42:2, 6-7

The journey of life is a series of moments in time and decisions. The ability to see past the immediate effect of your decision and how others will interpret it is a skill that can be acquired. This skill is called foresight. Foresight is the ability to use scenarios and critical thinking to predict what will happen. By utilizing experience, wisdom, and knowledge, you can calculate how a person may react to what you decide in any situation. Utilizing foresight can shift the questions you ask yourself when you have to choose in any situation. When you can anticipate the consequences of your choices, no longer will you ask the question,

"What can I experience now?" Instead, you will begin to think about "What will happen in one week, one year, or ten years?" Likewise, and more importantly, you will ask the questions:

Who will this affect?

Who is observing my choices?

What kind of ripples in fulfilling my purpose in the future will the choices I make now cause?

Through this small shift in thought, your world becomes less about you and more about those around you. Living in the present but thinking about the future of who you will influence is where true growth occurs, and moving forward from what seems like an endless cycle of mistakes becomes possible. However, we must be careful not to focus completely on the future or we will miss the goodness of the moment. Remember, a balance is needed. Ancient philosopher Laozi words this idea of balance perfectly:

"If you are depressed, you are living in the past. If you are anxious, you are living in the future. If you are peace, you are living in the present."[28]

The process of gaining foresight can be difficult and most likely will require years of reflection, knowledge accumulation, and heartbreaking experiences. However, like with most things in life, if a stimulus or catalyst is used to change your thought pattern, then the time and energy expended in grieving can be drastically shortened.

A catalyst is a substance that increases the rate of a reaction without being changed itself. It works by lowering the activation energy needed to start the change. It is important in practical

---

[28] Sophie A. Melbourne, "7 Simple Steps to Start Being More Mindful," The Beautiful Existence, 24 May 2017, https://thebeautifulexistence.com/7-simple-steps-to-start-being-more-mindful/.

applications but can also be applied in our own lives. People love using this word within business circles, but I am not sure if many have truly analyzed the meaning. By applying this definition, we can discuss why finding your catalyst for change will be essential to your journey throughout life.

CATALYST FOR CHANGE

My teenage daughter is almost identical to me. We think alike, react the same in situations that bring about emotion, and even laugh the same. For nineteen years of her life, I have been able to anticipate what she will do before she even knows she is going to do it. This is possible not because of some prophetic gifting but because I have done those exact things before. Sure, things may be a little different in how they are executed but the notion is the same. Let me share an example.

I remember catching her one night coming back home after having snuck out. I knew something was off all evening, but I chose not to say anything. I told my daughter I was going to bed around 11 p.m. one night. Call it parental intuition or just simply knowing that she is my daughter, I walked to her room and opened the door after an hour of some fake snoring from my bedroom. As I suspected, nobody was there. Now, most parents would panic. I smiled and thought about just how fun this lesson would be. Now, I am going to start with the statement, "I was mad!" I wanted to call her immediately and have her come back home. I even thought about going to get her, but I planned something different. As she was out partying, I was waiting at the exact location she used to make her escape. I was quietly watching clip after clip on YouTube while I waited. I sat patiently in the dark with a smirk on my face knowing that I had more experience in life than my daughter and, yet again, I was going to teach her a lesson. Time marched on and as minutes became hours, the anticipation was killing me. I wasn't worried about her. I knew she would be back. The anticipation came from the opportunity to demonstrate my knowledge and wisdom on something that she truly thought I would not know. More importantly, I thought about how I could teach her a lesson about life before it really mattered in the years that would follow.

I heard the car creep into the driveway, and she was home. She was so quiet as to not disturb anyone and just when she thought she got away with it, I turned the light on, turned the chair around, and said (as Dr. Evil would), "Hello Ms. Finley, welcome to my lair. I hope you had a great night because the punishment begins immediately as I feed you to Sansa." By the way, I took an empty paper towel roll, wrapped it in aluminum foil, and put it on Sansa's head to mimic a laser. She laughed; I laughed; but when the phone went away for three weeks, there was no laughing. She needed to learn a lesson and the catalyst of losing her phone made her think twice about doing it again. I can gladly say that never happened again. Dad-1: Daughter-0.

In the scenario above, the catalyst of change was minimal and without long-term consequences. The loss of the phone did not change the structure of the phone. It caused an emotional reaction within my daughter that was amplified by the loss of the phone. This, by definition, is a catalyst for change, not only in behavior but in mindset. Remember, a catalyst has to speed up a reaction, or, in this case, a lesson of life without being changed or exhausted itself.

Likewise, the catalyst that brought change to me was the thought about how I would be remembered. What legacy was I leaving to those around me? Was I going to leave a legacy that would be remembered by my children's children and generations after? If I was on the outside looking in, could I hold my head up high knowing that I made the right decisions in the life I was given? When I honestly asked myself these questions, I realized that my own life had to change. I realized that what I stood for had to become the very foundation on which my character would be built upon. That is how I wanted to be remembered, but how could I get there?

IMMEDIATE CIRCLE

The world is a big place. As of the year 2023, there are just over eight billion people. Social media, YouTube, and other advances in technology seem to have made the world a much smaller place. However, as the world appears smaller, a paradox has developed. Is it possible that the digital connections of our relationships may have become so large that we no longer have true relationships?

Robin Dunbar is a British evolutionary psychologist. His work has become famous and quoted in movies and books. Dr. Dunbar proposed a theory called the social brain hypothesis. According to this theory, a person can only have around 150 meaningful connections with others at any given time. A meaningful connection would be classified as a relationship that is deemed significant. It includes mutual respect, trust, and making a person feel valued. Based on the theory's findings, it has taken 150 people for a village to thrive throughout history.[29] In today's modern society, organizations have begun to explore the validity of this number today in our current societal constructs. For example, many companies have arranged their office spaces to adhere to this number, as they have found that when more employees are present, the best work is completed with fewer social problems developing within the office. Likewise, military analysts have studied this number to understand unit morale and the ability to execute leaders' orders with limited social pushback. Whether this is accurate down to an exact number is quite honestly irrelevant; however, what it does show is that despite our growing or shrinking world, a person can only process and maintain so many relationships because of limited physical, emotional, and mental bandwidth.

Equally as important as the 150 meaningful connections, Dr. Dunbar also stated that other social relationship numbers are nested within our social brain. What this means is that each layer of our interaction and connection to others, from the most intimate connection to a total stranger, increases by multiples of three. He stated that a person can have five loved ones, fifteen good friends/loved ones, fifty friends/good friends/loved ones, 150 meaningful connections, 500 acquaintances, and 1,500 people you recognize.[30]

Dr. Dunbar's research is fascinating to me. Although the numbers can vary at times throughout our lives, objective data that supports how we interact with other people in the world can be valuable within the right context. It showed me that

---

29 Robin I.M. Dunbar, "The Social Brain Hypothesis and Human Evolution," Oxford Research Encyclopedia of Psychology, 13, no. 44 (March 2016), https://www.doi.org/10.1093/acrefore/9780190236557.013.44.
30 Dunbar, "The Social Brain Hypothesis."

very few people will care about what we do on a personal level. So, who was I trying to impress? One last conclusion worth mentioning is that despite recognizing 1,500 people, you tend to devote two-thirds of your available social time to just fifteen individuals.

Fifteen people! I know what you are saying right now. "I am much more important than those numbers." Perhaps you are and perhaps you aren't, perhaps you have millions of followers on Instagram and companies pay you for your ability to influence those around you. Sure, people are easily influenced, and marketers have been using a psychological trick for years called social proof. It means that if people think everyone is doing it or using it, it must be right. Regardless—and I'm not going down that path in this book—ask yourself how many true relationships you have by thinking about what would happen on the day you die. More importantly, who would be at your funeral? I know this is morbid, but it will happen to us all one day. So, before you start, remember to be honest with yourself. Ask six questions:

Question 1: Who is there?

Question 2: Who planned your funeral?

Question 3: Who is crying?

Question 4: Who offered condolences to your family survivors?

Question 5: Who is there for the food?

Question 6: Who is sending their thoughts and prayers on Facebook?

Question 7: Who read about the news of your death, thought about how tragic it was, and just carried on with their day?

> IT WAS AT THAT MOMENT THAT I REALIZED THE CIRCLE OF THOSE I WANTED TO INFLUENCE MUST SHRINK.

My guess is you already know the answer to these questions. For the majority of you, your first answer will show your inflated self-worth or your lack of self-worth. For the remaining questions, the answers in numeric value would be five, fifteen, fifty, 150, 500, and 1,500 people, respectively. So, I asked the question, why do I truly give a rat's a** about what so many other people think about me? I give so little emotional/physical/mental time to so many people, so why should I allow their opinions to mean so much to me? It was at that moment that I realized the circle of those I wanted to influence must shrink. I determined I was going to devote my social energy and legacy-building to those who would be crying at my funeral. When I made this decision, my selfish ambition or visions of grandeur no longer held power over me. I was going to build a legacy concentrated on only those to whom I freely wanted to devote a large piece of my time. By narrowing my focus to good friends and those I loved, I was able to push through some "holdups" keeping me from growing. This decision was my catalyst.

HOW WOULD I BE REMEMBERED?

Who do you want to be? This is a simple question that, for some reason, we try to complicate. The answer to this question is what you wake up for every morning. Do you wake up to be the best in your profession? Are you trying to be the best manager, director, or executive? What happens when you die? Do you think you will be remembered for years to come? How about six months later? I can assure you that life and your business will move on fairly quickly, so to me, it seems like a waste of time to live for that reason.

Do you wake up to make a difference in people you have never met, or are you an entrepreneur trying to make a name for yourself? Once again, what happens when you die? I can assure you none of that will matter. So why do we do it?

> USE YOUR MISTAKES, SUCCESSES, AND INFLUENCE TO SHOW THOSE WHO CARE ABOUT YOU THAT YOU CARE FOR THEM.

We do it because we have no inkling of what we are doing in this life. We have let the world influence us on matters it does not understand and unfortunately, that mindset locks us into a cycle that keeps us unfulfilled. Be remembered as a man who lived life his way for the sake of others. Be remembered as a person who tried to make the lives of those he loved just a little better. Use your mistakes, successes, and influence to show those who care about you that you care for them. Show them the way to victory through your actions and wisdom on things you have experienced. Be known for your strong character, keep your word at all costs, and pursue things that are greater than you. Your actions today may lead to things you may never see the result of, but those results may come from your children instructing their children and many generations after because of a decision you made that began a legacy. It is hard to cut the grass in the dark, unable to relish in the satisfaction of seeing your work line by line, but it may be something that you are convicted to do. For me, I decided how I want to be remembered.

I want to be the catalyst for my family to change. I was going to stop trying to influence the world or seek approval from it. The reality that the world doesn't care about my life nor my feelings has never been truer. However, what the world doesn't know is that I don't really care. That is freedom. Freedom to make my life my own. Freedom to walk in who God created me to be. Freedom to build a legacy. Freedom to live the most rewarding life that I can live knowing that I overcame some really bad habits and mindsets. Despite my daily struggle with the ripples and scars of my actions, I am reassured that I have gained the wisdom to help those who mean the most to me. I hope that by prevailing through the dark times, I can instruct others to avoid the same mistakes I made.

CONCLUSION

If I was asked the age-old question, "Would you do things differently if you had the chance?" The immediate response would be yes.

I would not have hurt anyone. I would be grateful to have learned the lessons faster to save the time I spent pursuing things that were never meant for me. However, my delayed response would be no. The ability to tell this story is greater than my own. Sure, it may not be pretty to look at, but it was mine, and nobody can take that away from me. For the longest time, I was busy fighting to break free from my complicated life but now realize that I can use my mistakes to hopefully inspire those around me. After years of being burned out, stressed out, and constantly reverting, little did I realize the key to freedom was changing my focus and fighting for my legacy within my immediate circle. Fighting for something so simple—what I was going to leave behind to my family and friends—is a much stronger motivator than trying to change the world. If you are a military man, remember this: Stop looking down the gun barrel when you enter the room. This is too narrow a focus. Likewise, stop looking at the whole building before you decide what direction to go. This is too broad a focus. Instead, look around in your immediate area with your eyes open. I believe you will find the problem is not so big when you just change your perspective.

AFTERWORD

Remember, worlds will always collide.

My son, do not reject or take lightly the discipline of the Lord [learn from your mistakes and the testing that comes from His correction through discipline]; nor despise His rebuke, For those whom the Lord loves He corrects, even as a father corrects the son in whom he delights. —Proverbs 3:11-12 (AMP)

Running is a very demanding sport on both the body and mind. In the US, it is estimated that about fifty million people (or 15 percent) of the population would identify themselves as a runner. The reason for their running can vary from weight loss to achieving a daily goal that helps create happiness. Throughout the world, thousands of clubs have been created to appeal to runners. Billions of marketing dollars have been spent creating a culture surrounding the activity of running. Although the natural tendency of the human body is to move, running might not be your thing. Some people are built to glide and others just plop. Gliders are those people whom you never have to guess if they run;; they will make sure to tell you. On the other hand, ploppers are the ones whose knees hurt just from the thought of running. Ploppers are the ones who say quirky things along the lines of how they would only run if someone was chasing them. Regardless of your opinion on running, let's take away the physical component of it for a minute. The piece remaining is the psychological aspect of it, and that is not always a good thing.

A person's natural instinct is to run when things get hard. An entire autonomic nervous system was built for this sole purpose. The ole "fight or flight" sympathetic nervous system is a powerful force that will dictate your thoughts and actions based upon chemical releases in the brain triggered by experiences or memories. When this system is triggered, what you do is a collection of decisions both conscious and unconscious. However, there are some things that you cannot run from no matter how painful it may be. You could run from one end of the world to the other, and that would not be far enough.

For every action, there is a reaction. With every decision you have made in the past, that decision will affect the outcome of your present and future to some degree. The size of the effect is determined by time but also by how you have grown and learned from what you experienced in the past. I wish I could say that once you learn from a mistake, you can ride off into the sunset free of any chance of regression. Unfortunately, you will be tested over and over again to see that you have truly learned your lesson. It is a tragedy that it's not more simple than that, but the reason for this is that the strings of your life have been interwoven amongst society.

Some people have known you during the darkest of times and others are meeting you for the first time. The scars of your past are a part of you. There may be things that you never want to talk about again, but those things have a way of finding you whether you try to run from them or ignore them. When you least expect it, your past will come back to you at the most unexpected time. You have to be prepared to give an answer to the hope that is inside you. You have to be prepared to explain what brought you to the place you are now. Despite knowing this, you can't be afraid to start over. This time you're not starting from scratch; you're starting from experience. The more you have grown, the better your reset can be. People will either accept you for who you are now, or they will not. That decision is not for you to worry about, as you are to base your life on your purpose and not performance.

THE LIFE OF JEAN VALJEAN

As I close this book, let me share one last story with you about a seed that was planted and began to grow before I could even comprehend its meaning. When I was in the ninth grade, my school required every student to take a foreign language. While Spanish seemed like the logical choice, for some odd reason (the girls took this class),), I decided to take French. What I learned in those years is just a memory, but an experience has resonated inside of me in the years that have followed.

Growing up in New Jersey, we lived about forty-five minutes from New York City. On a cold December night, crammed in a "short" yellow school bus, the ninth-grade French class got to attend a Broadway play. For an awkward, skinny, short, blonde-haired boy, this would be my first Broadway experience. To keep with the French theme, that play was *Les Misérables*.[31] This acclaimed theatrical masterpiece was a rendition of Victor

---
31 Victor Hugo, Les Misérables.

Hugo's work first published in 1862.³² It depicts the life of Jean Valjean and his desire to live a normal life despite being labeled a dangerous prisoner, serving nineteen years for stealing a loaf of bread for his starving sister and her son. The story begins with his release from prison and culminates in his death. What happens throughout the novel has been labeled the greatest literary work of the nineteenth century depicting human nature, the concepts of right and wrong, and the fallacy of perceived belief in the inability to change.

As you sit and watch, almost immediately, the story takes its first twist upon an act of kindness that Jean Valjean encounters from a Bishop of the Catholic church, Bienvenue. Within the first scenes of the book, Jean Valjean was starving, beaten down, and without hope. He had succumbed to being a criminal as the world had labeled him. In believing this, Jean Valjean stole silver from the church where he was being sheltered as a guest and departed in the night. When the authorities brought Jean Valjean back to the bishop, anticipating him to say that the silver was stolen, Bienvenue saw Jean Valjean for who he was and not as who the world labeled him to be. Seeing his true soul, Bienvenue offers Jean Valjean the finest silver candlesticks and upon his physical release, states he needs to use this silver to become an honorable man, but more importantly, he has saved his soul for God.

At this point, Jean Valjean begins his internal battle. He wrestles with his anger, the darkness of his thoughts, and his belief that he is a thief in the night, as he has been told this constantly for twenty years. In this battle raging inside, he begins to express shame and doubt. As the scene continues, he travels to the lowest

---

32 Victor Hugo, "Les Misérables" in Les Misérables (Belgium, Ger: A. Lacroix, Verboeckhoven & Cie, 1862).

point within himself, and remembering the kindness and love he experienced, Jean Valjean rises out of his mental prison, walks out of the church in a triumphant decree through a graveyard, and declares he is no longer Jean Valjean, and another story must begin. He realizes that who he thinks he is or what he thinks of the world are stories he has told himself but are not who he actually is. So, in the final part of the scene, he gloriously declares his story will be written by God as he stands next to a cross, signifying his resurrection.

Many years go by, and we see Jean Valjean now using an alias. He has become a wealthy, kind, and generous city mayor. However, despite his obvious radical transformation and changed beliefs of himself and the world, he couldn't run from the past. Enter the protagonist of the story. Inspector Javert is a man of the law. He believes in the law completely and believes that if a person is once a criminal, they will always be a criminal. Throughout the novel, Javert continuously pursues the criminal Jean Valjean over many decades until an end decisively culminates.

> TRUE TRANSFORMATION CANNOT AND DOES NOT ABSOLVE A PERSON FROM THEIR SINS OR CRIMES OF THE PAST.

Jean Valjean is now an old man by nineteenth-century standards. In an act of mercy during the June Rebellion, or the Paris Uprising of 1832, Jean Valjean spares Inspector Javert's life from those who would have him dead. Coming full circle, it was Javert who was now shown an act of kindness. Like Jean Valjean, Javert must now decide what to do with this act of kindness and what to do now that his worldview has been challenged. Javert is stuck in a dilemma of opposing realities. On one hand, if what Javert believes is true, people cannot change, and he should be dead. However, if what Javert believes is untrue and people can change, then his past self must die. So, in a melancholy moment at rock bottom, instead of taking the leap of faith to resurrection, Javert leaps off a bridge to death to escape the world of Jean Valjean.

By reading this novel or watching this movie or play, we are strongly reminded of one truth that cannot be avoided. There is no such thing as a spiritual bypass. True transformation cannot and does not absolve a person from their sins or crimes of the past. A person must face their past despite what consequences may follow by revealing who they were. True transformation cannot be completed until a person can make amends with both himself and those who have been wronged, despite potential loss of love, job, or life in the face of opposing views. Transformation can only be achieved when you hit bottom in your old life and are able to non-defensively reveal your past self when confronted or challenged in your new life.

IT IS WORTH THE FIGHT

John Stuart Mill, a nineteenth-century British philosopher writes:

> *War is an ugly thing, but not the ugliest of things. The decayed and degraded state of moral and patriotic feeling which thinks that nothing is worth war is much worse. A man who has nothing for which he is willing to fight,*

nothing which is more important than his own personal safety, is a miserable creature and has no chance of being free unless made and kept so by the exertions of better men than himself.[33]

Each person has to decide what they are willing to fight for. Each person has been placed in this world for a very specific reason. Those who are unwilling to accept the need to fight for something greater than themselves are summed up above as "miserable creatures."

When we think of the word "fighting," a range of thoughts can flood our minds—fear, pain, anxiety, anger, or rage, to name a few. Whatever word we associate with a fight is largely based on our experience and what the fight is about. If the fight is over something we perceive as wrong, then anger coupled with fear might prevail. If we are fighting for selfish reasons, then rage and anxiety may prevail. One thing that remains the same is that the purpose of a fight is a means to achieve an end.

> WHEN YOU STAND FOR SOMETHING YOU TRULY BELIEVE IN, THE FIGHT WILL COME TO YOU.

Fighting is defined as designed, intended, or trained for combat. Training for combat is an interesting way to think about fighting. The Chinese proverb that writes "It's better to be a warrior in a

---
33 John Stuart Mill, Principles of Political Economy (United Kingdom: John W. Parker, 1848).

garden than a gardener in a war" tells us something quite important. It is important to prepare for what is coming to you. It is important to be able to defend yourself and understand the strategy of the enemy you may be facing. When you stand for something you truly believe in, the fight will come to you. No hiding, running, or pretending that it will never happen to you will keep you safe. This is important to understand so that you are ready to face it.

Over the course of this book, I have outlined Ten Hard Facts. If you have experienced any of them, you will have to fight for something greater than yourself to achieve victory over your problem. To believe or hope that someone will achieve victory for you is just a foolish notion. There is no counselor, significant other, or friend that can fight these battles for you. You must be willing to stand firm despite the hardship or backlash you will face when you begin to change course toward your purpose in life. There is nothing more fearful for your enemy than having the conviction to achieve a greater purpose than yourself.

THE CAVE

Before you can prepare to fight for your purpose and make your stand for what you believe in, there will be a period of time or season that you will have to endure. I like to refer to this as cave time. I am not referring to your Man Cave time. This is not the time when you get to watch football and shoot pool. The time I am talking about is the time when you take a step back from the world. This is step back must happen so that you can begin to understand your worth with outside influence. This can range from living in the woods for months, to traveling abroad, to committing to cutting away things that have caused you to stumble in the past. Whatever the source of your issues, you have to take a step back and essentially hide for some time. Oh, I understand every one of us has obligations. If the problem is work, you just can't get up and leave for a month or two (or so you think).If the problem is a woman, you can't just cut off communication for a season . . . or can you?

The cave will look different for all of us. The point is that you have to dissociate from certain things in order to change your course. You have to give yourself the time needed to work through your loss or emotions and regain your common sense of what you know to be true. It took me disappearing for one month with Sansa to regain focus and understand my next steps and what I had to do. I left everything behind during that time—my job, relationships, and obligations. When I came out of my cave, I had a renewed sense of what was important and went to work, cutting away all the things that were holding me back from my true self. I wish I could say that it was instant. Like most things, not a chance. It took years to finish cleaning up the messes I created but I will say that it was the steps of faith toward a greater purpose that exponentially drove the change.

It Will Never End, but It Will Get Easier

Inside of us, there will always be a battle. The battle of what we experienced, what we believe to be true, and what is actually true, whether we experienced it or not. As Mark Twain once wrote, "It ain't what you don't know that gets you into trouble. It's what you know for sure that just ain't so."[34]

---

34 Mark Twain, "It ain't what you don't know that gets you into trouble. It's what you know for sure that just ain't so," Goodreads, https://www.goodreads.com/quotes/7588008-it-ain-t-what-you-don-t-know-that-gets-you-into.

Each and every one of us has lived, is living, and will live our own lives. My life will never be yours, and yours will never be mine. What works for me may not work for you. People around you might not understand what it is you have to do to gain freedom over what has bothered you for so long. Our experiences help mold us into who we are, but they do not define us. Our truth gives us meaning for what we do, but that doesn't mean it defines us. In this world, truth is rarely discussed. Some people say there is no absolute truth in this world. However, that statement is made with a statement of an absolute truth to refute the existence of an absolute truth. The point is that there has to be a truth or there can be no trust. Without trust, there can be no purpose, as your life is what it is strictly by chance. Search for the truth in your actions, and you will know you are on the right path when you have a sense of peace and fulfillment. Without that, you are just living life.

As you go further and further in the right direction of who you were created to be, you will find that your steps become easier and easier to take. You will begin to recognize in others where you have been, and that positive reinforcement will help you take the next step. Be careful not to become prideful; remember, it wasn't too long ago when you started the journey.

LIFE IS NOT A COOKBOOK

In the introduction, I mentioned that there is no specific way to live life. I hope by now you realize the accuracy of that statement. I went through challenge after challenge, and by no means are the challenges over. I don't know what will happen to me or what I will have to face day to day. Some days are better than others, but it is understanding where I have been and putting my hope in the truth of knowing where I am going that drives me forward. I am sure that I will make another mistake at some point, but I believe that by knowing and experiencing what I have, the bottom of that mistake will not be nearly as deep or devastating.

As the end of this story draws near, it is my hope that these lessons will have moved you to action. The action you may take will determine your life for years to come. Perhaps you are moved to terminate a relationship that you have been too afraid to leave. Perhaps you are afraid of leaving that dead-end job because you have no idea where the money will come from. Even still, perhaps you doubt who you think you can be because you have believed what others have said about who they think you are for so long that you could never believe anything else. WRONG!! You are who your Creator says that you are. It is time to dig deep down and pull yourself out of the shithole you have created for yourself. It will be painful when you reverse course. Your emotions and truth will be tested when you begin to cut things out of your life that do not belong. It will get harder the more you train for the fight which will ultimately lead you to find your purpose. It will be lonely standing for what you believe in to those around you. However, if you endure the mocking, trials, and setbacks, you will find serenity despite the world around you. If you succeed, you will have done something that very few have the courage to see through to completion. If you walk your journey to completion, you will understand something deeper about yourself and about those around you. What you do with that knowledge and wisdom is the topic of another book. The world desperately needs to read this other book—YOUR book, replete with your own story—to continue the conversation that will break the chains off so many others in bondage. Take care, my friends, and may the grace and favor of the Lord be upon you, your family, and your life's voyage.

www.ingramcontent.com/pod-product-compliance
Lightning Source LLC
Chambersburg PA
CBHW071215100426
42735CB00048B/3024